THE

EXECUTIVE

SCALPEL

Cutting Through The Business Of Medicine

The Healthcare Provider's Guide To Success

Dr. Justin Sherfey

Beyond Ordinary Publications, LLC

© 2025 Beyond Ordinary Publications, LLC

Printed in the United States of America

ISBN: 979-8-9999241-0-0

LCCN: 2025925035

BEYOND ORDINARY PUBLICATIONS LLC

Special Thanks

Thank you to my wife, Debrah. Her unwavering support and encouragement have shaped every step of my journey. It's true that behind every good man is a better woman, and I am living proof.

Thank you to my Mom and Dad. You gave me the foundation and faith that my life is built on. Dad, with your MBA training and years of real-world entrepreneurial experience, you taught me how to be a business leader, and a critical thinker. Thank you for the countless hours of encouragement, editing, and feedback that made this book possible.

Thank you to my son and daughter-in-law, Nathan and Vanessa, and to my daughter, Jordan. You are each an incredible blessing, and I learn from you every day. Jordan, your insights as a healthcare professional, along with your feedback and editing, helped move this book from vision to reality. Nathan, your MBA training and management experience have given me the valuable perspective of a young business leader.

Thank you to my brother, Dr. Michael Sherfey, and my sister, Dr. Heather Preissler, for their feedback and input to improve the book content and make the message relevant.

Special thanks to my friend and business partner, Dr. Tom Nasser. This book would not exist without the hard-earned lessons we learned together in the trenches of starting, running, and growing a practice, and a business.

This book is a result of love and support that only family and friends can provide.

Table of Contents

Forward

Certain professions still carry a sacred weight, firefighters, police officers, military personnel, and physicians are among them. These roles don't just require skill; they require sacrifice, conviction, and a deep sense of calling. When you enter one of these fields, you are not simply taking a job. You are accepting a mantle. You are pledging your life in service of something greater than yourself. For the firefighter, it means running into burning buildings. For the police officer, it means standing in the line of fire.

And for the physician, it means placing the lives of others, strangers, above your own. It's not glamorous. It's not easy. But it's necessary. *"You are the salt of the earth. But if the salt loses its saltiness, how can it be made salty again? It is no longer good for anything, except to be thrown out and trampled underfoot."* - Matthew 5:13

Jesus' words speak directly to the soul of our profession. Salt preserves. Salt seasons. Salt purifies. But when it loses its potency, it's cast aside, rendered useless. And the same is happening in medicine. We're watching an industry, once deeply rooted in human connection and sacred trust, begin to lose its saltiness. Not because we've lost our intelligence, but because we've lost our grit, our zeal, and perhaps most dangerously, our autonomy. We entered this field with passion. But bureaucracy has dulled it.

We once saw patients as sacred trusts. Now they are often seen as "throughput." We once answered our calling. Now we often answer to administrators, algorithms, and insurance companies.

And if we, as physicians, don't fight to preserve the saltiness of this profession, its purpose, its dignity, and its soul, then it will be non-physicians who dictate how we care for people. The result? A fragmented, soulless machine. Patients suffer. Doctors burn out. Trust erodes.

That's why this book matters. It's not just another voice in the chaos; it's a call back to who we are. A reminder of why we started. A plea to rekindle the fire. The author doesn't merely describe the decline; he challenges it. He calls us to be bold, to reclaim the values that once defined this noble profession. I've been a physician for over two decades. I've led departments, walked with patients through pain and healing, and watched our field evolve. I've seen doctors lose their joy. I've seen others rise above the noise and become beacons. This book reminds us that we have a choice: to be bland or to be salt.

If you've felt disillusioned, this book is for you.

If you've felt the fire flickering, this book is for you.

If you still believe medicine can be a holy, healing, and human endeavor, this book is definitely for you. And perhaps one of the strongest things we can do to preserve our autonomy and ability to care for the desperate humans who need us most is to learn not just how to function in the business of medicine, but how to thrive in it. This book contains what many seasoned physicians would recognize as the hard-won secrets and key ingredients to navigating that beautiful, adventurous journey. In the end, I hope you find it to be the same wonderful and rewarding experience it has been for me and for so many others who have chosen to embark on the tumultuous road of private practice. After all, what is life and what is a career if we don't challenge ourselves to reach the summit of every experience?

We didn't come this far, just to come this far.

T. S. Nasser, D.O., FAAPMR
Physician. Father. Follower of Christ.
October 2025

Introduction

Why should you listen to me?

I didn't write this book because I discovered all the answers or cracked the code to effortless success. I wrote it because I have lived the struggles that many healthcare professionals silently endure. I witnessed friends, colleagues, and even mentors work themselves to the point of complete burnout, chasing an elusive vision of success that always seemed just out of reach. Too often, these bright and dedicated individuals found themselves exhausted, frustrated, and asking, "Is this all there is?"

I understand that feeling because I've been there too.

My journey into medicine wasn't exactly typical; it was a winding, difficult path full of unexpected detours and hard lessons. (For the full story, I invite you to read Appendix 1.) Due to my path, I developed a perspective that is slightly different from the traditional narrative we hear in our training and early careers. I didn't follow a perfect, straight line to a dream job or an easy leadership role. Instead, I stumbled, learned the hard way, adapted, and eventually found a way not only to survive but to thrive in the complex world of healthcare.

What motivated me to write this, though, wasn't just the success. It was watching colleagues, good people, talented physicians, work themselves into the ground only to reach their 60s or 70s and realize they don't have the financial security to retire comfortably. That's heartbreaking, and it's avoidable. I don't claim to have all the answers, but I do believe I've walked a path that others can learn from. I'm not here to pretend I know everything. No one does. There is no magic formula that guarantees instant success in medicine, either clinically or on the business side of healthcare. However, what I can offer are hard-won lessons that I wish someone had taught me when I was struggling. I want to share strategies, mindsets, and techniques that can save you years of wasted effort, endless frustration, and sleepless nights.

This book is about the business of medicine, a topic that often feels taboo, misunderstood, or secondary during medical training. Yet it's one of the most critical areas that determines whether you'll find lasting success and satisfaction in your career. Understanding the business side isn't about "selling out" or prioritizing profit over patients; it's about protecting your ability to care for patients while also building a sustainable, rewarding life for yourself. It's about learning to navigate the complex, ever-changing healthcare system in a way that opens doors rather than closes them.

Healthcare is a notoriously challenging industry. Red tape, bureaucracy, changing regulations, and financial pressures can make even the most dedicated physician feel powerless. But I'm here to tell you: opportunity is everywhere if you know where and how to look.

This book is my attempt to give you a roadmap, based not on theory but on real-world experience. I want you to avoid some of the mistakes I made. I want to show you how to recognize hidden opportunities, make informed decisions, and build a career that offers not just professional success but also personal fulfillment.

This book is organized into three sections that serve as a roadmap to help guide you toward success. The first section offers background and examines the significant challenges facing healthcare today. The second section lays out essential business foundations and strategies for growth. The final section focuses on the key people, parts, and principles that will propel you to lasting success.

Whether you're just starting your journey or years into practice and wondering how to reclaim your passion, I hope the pages that follow will help you see a bigger picture and remind you that success in the business of medicine is not only possible but well within your reach.

Let's get started.

Part One:

Background and Challenges

*What does it profit a man to gain the whole world, yet
forfeit his soul?*

(Mark 8:36)[1]

---

[1] The Holy Bible, New International Version. Grand Rapids: Zondervan, 2011. Mark 8:36.

Chapter 1:
Roadmap to Success

There is no magic formula for success in healthcare. And the way to achieve it is not one-size-fits-all. What works for one practice may not work for another, depending on factors such as location, patient population, provider personality, market forces, and numerous other variables. But there are proven strategies and unique ways to maximize your chances of success. One important thing to understand from the start is that no "business strategy" will ever replace the need to practice high-quality medicine with caring and compassion. If you consistently treat your patients with skill, integrity, and empathy, you can have a successful and fulfilling career. That being said, this foundation, while critical, is only one part of the puzzle. The reality of modern healthcare is that running a practice is no longer just about being a good doctor. It requires a whole other set of skills and knowledge that, unfortunately, many of us were never taught.

Most of my colleagues, and many of the physicians or healthcare providers I meet or interact with regularly, are highly intelligent, hardworking, and deeply committed to their patients. But when it comes to the business side of medicine, many are unfortunately quite ignorant. And I don't use that word in a judgmental way, I mean it in the literal sense: they simply haven't had the education or exposure to understand how to run a business effectively.

Medical school doesn't prepare you for this. Residency doesn't teach you how to read a P&L statement, negotiate a payer contract, structure a compensation model, or build a brand. Much of the system appears to be set up to discourage physicians from learning these things, as if taking an interest in the business side somehow makes one less devoted to patient care. That couldn't be further from the truth. Taking control of the business aspects of your practice allows you to protect your ability to provide excellent care on your terms, rather than being forced to compromise due to financial pressure or administrative demands.

Some providers do manage to piece together a basic understanding. Maybe they've attended a few lectures at a conference, read a book or two, or taken advice from a successful colleague. Those are all helpful starting points, and they can shape your vision for your practice. My goal here is to build on that foundation by sharing insights derived from real-world experience, not theory, but rather trial and error, wins and losses, and ultimately help you build something sustainable and scalable. There are no guarantees in this space, but I want to give you a practical framework, rooted in what has worked for me and others like me.

At the time I'm writing this, my practice includes over fifteen providers and employs more than 150 people. We have multiple ancillary revenue streams, including imaging, physical therapy, outpatient surgery, medical equipment, and more. We've built a network of interconnected business entities that support one another, encompassing billing and marketing as well as management services. The practice has designed a corporate structure that provides legal and financial protection. In addition, retirement planning is embedded directly into the business, allowing both partners and employees to build long-term security through their work. These aren't things that happened overnight. Each piece took time, investment, setbacks, and strategic decisions. And yet, it's all possible, a testament not just to the model we've built but to the structure and value behind it.

If sharing what I've done helps even a few people avoid burnout, grow stronger businesses, and enjoy the kind of freedom that lets them practice on their terms, then this effort will have been worthwhile.

ROADMAP to SUCCESS

SUCCESS

PARTS, PEOPLE & PRINCIPLES

- ↑ End of Status Quo
- ↑ The Team
- ↑ Matter of Principle
- ↑ Leadership
- ↑ Stuck in the System
- ↑ Final Thoughts

FOUNDATIONS & STRATEGIES

- ↑ The Right Structure
- ↑ You're Worth a Lot
- ↑ Don't Work for Free
- ↑ Play with the Big Boys
- ↑ Ancillary Streams
- ↑ Tech Toys
- ↑ Let's Make a Deal
- ↑ Virtual World
- ↑ Opportunities
- ↑ Providers at All Levels

BACKGROUND & CHALLENGES

- ↑ Roadmap to Success
- ↑ The Calling
- ↑ The Choices
- ↑ Sterotypes
- ↑ Headaches
- ↑ Guilt
- ↑ The Barriers

Take Care of YOUR PATIENTS

Do Not be Afraid to Fail.

VALUE YOUR TIME!

Chapter 2:
The Calling

To become a doctor has been a parent's dream for their children for as long as I can remember. In some cultures, it is one of the highest positions of honor one can aim for. The thought of being a healer and having such an influence on someone's life can be very alluring to one's sense of purpose. Some people have felt a calling to this profession from a very young age. A sense of duty embedded deep within their soul, a yearning to help those in need, to ease suffering, to mend what is broken, and to be a source of comfort for those who are hurting. These individuals may have started on the pathway to medicine with clear goals and unwavering determination, driven by an innate desire to become the practitioners they are destined to be. Their focus, dedication, and passion have propelled them forward, making the sacrifices of long nights, endless studying, and the emotional toll of medicine seem worth the cost.

Others saw the career as one that came with prestige, a title that commanded admiration, and perhaps a sense of power. A physician is a position of authority, an individual to whom people turn in times of vulnerability, placing their trust and well-being in their hands. It carries the societal recognition and the ability to stand at the intersection of science and human compassion.

Many view medicine as a gateway to stability, a career that offers security and financial rewards. In a world where change is constant and industries fluctuate, healthcare remains an ever-present necessity. The promise of a secure income, the potential for financial growth, and the knowledge that doctors will always be needed have made the profession appealing to many who seek economic stability.

For some, the influence of a mentor, a family member, or a personal experience within the healthcare system guided their decision. A close interaction with a doctor who made a lasting impact, a family member's illness that inspired a sense of duty, or a moment of realization that they, too, could make a difference in people's lives. These experiences serve as a foundation, a source of motivation that fuels the journey toward becoming a physician. It is the desire to give back, to provide the same level of care and compassion that was once received, that pushes them forward.

I had none of these. I consider my path to medicine to be atypical, shaped by trial and error, with unexpected turns, and a series of moments ultimately leading me to discover a career that aligned with my natural abilities. I had no family members or friends in the medical field, nor did I have a childhood dream of wearing a white coat or holding a stethoscope. My upbringing was steeped in business and management, a world where numbers, strategy, and leadership produced success. My parents encouraged me to find my path, but medicine was never a consideration. When my father once suggested it as a possible direction for my studies, I was strongly opposed to the idea. The thought of dealing with the sick, the injured, or those in pain was not something I felt drawn to. The idea of being surrounded by illness, of bearing the weight of responsibility for another's well-being, was daunting. It was a world that I neither understood nor wanted to be a part of.

I actively avoided anything related to medicine, steering clear of hospitals, medical discussions, and situations where I might be required to confront suffering. It was not out of fear, but rather a lack of connection to the field. I saw myself in a different realm, perhaps in business like my family, navigating corporate structures, managing enterprises, or creating something innovative. My mind was set on a future that did not include the medical world, and I was confident in that decision. But life, as it often does, had other plans for me.

The doorway to medicine did not swing open for me grandly or profoundly. It was not an epiphany or a moment of revelation. It was a slow, gradual process, one that took time, small experiences, and a growing awareness of where my strengths lay.

Only when I began to engage with people in healthcare and see how knowledge could be applied in a way that directly impacted others, did my perspective start to shift. I realized that medicine was not solely about dealing with sickness or injury; it was about understanding, about connection, about the ability to take knowledge and use it in a way that made a tangible difference. It was about logic and structure, but also intuition and empathy. Slowly, my resistance changed into curiosity. I began to understand how medicine encompasses elements of problem-solving, critical thinking, and the ability to make decisions that impact real lives. I saw how it challenged both the mind and the heart, requiring not only intelligence but also resilience, adaptability, and a willingness to step into the unknown.

As I ventured further into this world, I found that my initial reservations had been based on misconceptions. Medicine is not constantly surrounded by suffering; it alleviates it. It is not about shouldering unbearable burdens; it is learning how to carry them in a way that makes a difference.

Looking back, I now see my path toward medicine was one of discovery. I did not follow the traditional routes of childhood aspiration, mentorship, or a single defining moment. Instead, I found my way to medicine through a journey that naturally unfolded in its own time. And on that journey, I learned that the best paths are often those we never planned for, the ones that surprise us, challenge us, and ultimately lead us to where we are meant to be.

Chapter 3: Stereotypes
The Helper and the Hero

Most medical professionals fall into two categories: The Helper or the Hero. Below, I discuss each category in turn.

The Helper

The Helper believes medicine is a calling. For them, medicine is more than just a career or a job; it is their life purpose. What drives the Helper is their desire to relieve suffering and heal sickness. As such, they do not measure success by financial gain or professional honors. Because the Helper believes medicine is a calling, they often enter the academic and research side of healthcare, dedicating their life to teaching future providers or advancing medical knowledge. Many Helpers feel compelled to serve underserved populations, where there is limited access to healthcare, or choose primary care, which enables them to form lasting relationships with their patients.

In contrast, others opt for specialty fields where they can fulfill their calling in a more focused capacity. Regardless of which path the Helper chooses, what motivates them is their unwavering sense of purpose. Their drive to serve the ill and injured stems from a profound sense of compassion and a moral obligation to use their skills for the greater good. While their motivation is a noble one, driving the Helper to become an exceptional caregiver, it can be a handicap when dealing with business and financial decisions.

One of the most significant obstacles the Helper faces is what I call the "Guilt of the Calling." This phenomenon arises when a provider feels an overwhelming sense of guilt or discomfort when considering financial matters related to their practice. The Helper feels conflicted when they are forced to discuss revenue, profitability, and compensation. Such topics are at odds with their altruistic motivation. For the Helper, the idea of profiting from healthcare feels morally wrong, as though placing a dollar value on their service somehow diminishes the purity of their calling. Such a mindset often leads to poor financial decisions, including undercharging for services, failing to enforce payment policies, and not discussing fees with patients upfront.

A common struggle the Helper faces is collecting unpaid invoices, sending patients to collections, and discontinuing treatment due to unpaid bills. The Helper can feel that enforcing such policies contradicts their purpose. Generosity and compassion are crucial in medicine, but not at the expense of sound business management. A medical practice, after all, is a business with employees to pay and operating costs to cover if it is to continue functioning. If the practice is financially unstable, it cannot continue to provide care, and ultimately, patients will suffer as a result.

I have worked with physicians who fit the Helper profile and have found that with guidance and training, they can be both great providers and successful business leaders. Their passion and calling can drive their success, provided they learn to balance their altruism with sound financial practices. A successful medical practice does not mean compromising one's ethics or mission; instead, it allows for greater flexibility in helping those in need. Financial stability provides the resources to fund pro bono work, support underserved communities, and invest in better equipment and staff, all of which benefit patients.

One physician colleague comes to mind when I think of the Helper. His father was an orthopedic surgeon, and this familial influence led him to pursue a career in orthopedic medicine. His father was also a passionate missionary in the medical field, regularly leading teams to foreign countries to perform joint replacements and other orthopedic procedures for those who otherwise would not have access to such care. Inspired by his father's work, this physician was deeply committed to helping his patients, often going above and beyond to ensure they received the needed care, regardless of their ability to pay.

His noble intentions sometimes clashed with the realities of running a medical practice. He struggled to enforce financial policies, hesitated to collect overdue payments, and often felt uneasy making decisions he perceived as prioritizing business over patient care. He disliked discussing financial matters with patients, believing it was inappropriate and fearing it might compromise his integrity as a healer.

Through extensive conversations and mentorship, he gradually came to understand that financial health and patient care are not mutually exclusive. By implementing structured financial policies and clear payment expectations, his practice remained financially solvent, and he expanded his ability to help others. With a stable practice, he could allocate resources for charity, participate in medical missions, and offer sliding-scale payment options for patients in need, all without jeopardizing the sustainability of his practice.

One of the key lessons Helpers must learn is that financial responsibility is not a sign of greed; it is a means of ensuring longevity and making a lasting impact. A well-run practice can employ more staff, invest in advanced technology, and treat a greater number of patients. When a practice is constantly struggling to stay afloat due to unpaid bills and financial mismanagement, it may be forced to shut its doors, leaving patients without access to care.

A crucial step to overcome the "Guilt of the Calling" is to reframe the way the Helper views financial discussions. These conversations should be viewed as a way to ensure fairness and sustainability, rather than as uncomfortable or unethical. Patients who can afford to pay should do so, as this allows the practice to continue serving those who genuinely cannot. Transparency in financial matters also fosters trust and ensures that patients understand the value of the care they receive. Finding the right balance between altruism and business acumen is essential for the Helper to thrive in medical practice.

Strategies for the Helper

Education on Business Fundamentals: Many medical professionals receive little to no training in business management during their education. Seeking mentorship, attending business workshops, and taking courses on medical practice management can be invaluable.

Setting Clear Financial Policies: Establish structured payment plans, clear billing procedures, and consistent policies regarding unpaid bills. This will eliminate ambiguity and reduce stress for both providers and patients.

Delegate Financial Responsibilities: Many Helpers benefit from hiring a trusted office manager or financial consultant who can handle billing and collections, allowing them to focus on patient care while ensuring the practice remains financially stable.

Reframe Financial Success: Recognizing that your profitable practice enables you to provide greater service to the community will alleviate feelings of guilt. A financially healthy practice can offer charitable services, hire needed staff, and provide better care.

Seek Support and Mentorship: Connect with like-minded professionals who have successfully balanced their calling with business success. They can provide valuable insights and encouragement.

The Helper's sense of purpose and passion are tremendous assets. These providers bring compassion, dedication, and an unwavering commitment to patient care to the medical profession. By learning to integrate sound business principles into their practice, they can enhance their ability to serve others while maintaining a sustainable and fulfilling career. Finding this balance is not easy, but it is possible, and when achieved, it leads to a truly impactful and rewarding medical career.

The Hero

The Hero is an individual who entered healthcare not only out of their desire to help others, but also for the prestige and personal validation that the title of Physician provides. The hero carries themselves with confidence, often bordering on arrogance. They assume they are the most intelligent person in the room. To the Hero, respect is not earned; it is assumed, and as such, their authority is beyond question.

This Hero is stereotypical of how the public often views the physician. Words like aloof, conceited, and narcissistic are frequently used adjectives when people speak of doctors they have encountered. Of course, it's never this black and white. Self-confidence is a vital trait for physicians, particularly surgeons. In the operating room with the scalpel in hand and a patient on the operating table, hesitation or self-doubt can be deadly. The ability to make quick, high-stakes decisions with conviction is crucial. This type of confidence is hard-earned and necessary. Like any strength left unchecked, self-confidence can become a liability. The Hero's confidence, if unbridled, can inflate the Hero's ego and affect their performance, especially when the needed confidence is not balanced with enough humility to be open to other perspectives. While the Hero's confidence enables them to trust their ability to save lives, it can also lead them to easily disregard the input from a colleague, a business advisor, or even their staff.

From a business standpoint, working with the Hero can be challenging. Their self-image can prevent them from accepting guidance, particularly in areas outside their expertise. Often, the Hero will bristle at the idea of being told what to do, especially from a person lacking letters after their name. The Hero's limited business knowledge, combined with their natural resistance to non-clinical leadership, can make them prone to poor decisions in managing the administrative and financial aspects of their practice. Heroes are often brilliant clinicians but ineffective leaders.

I've seen this often in my profession of orthopedic surgery. One colleague I worked with was an incredibly gifted surgeon. His knowledge of advanced techniques, combined with his confidence, yielded solid outcomes, and patients appreciated him in the operating room. However, his practice suffered financially due to outdated billing methods, high staff turnover, and his unwillingness to consider his office manager's suggestion to implement an updated electronic health record (EHR) system, as he did not see the value in the more expensive technology. Just because he had mastered the Operating Room, he felt he could master every other aspect of his business on his instinct alone.

His practice eventually began to lose money, despite high patient volume. Of course, as the Hero, he blamed insurance companies, staff inefficiency, and the local economy, but never himself. His practice did not begin to improve financially until he reluctantly brought in outside help.

Even then, he battled each change. It took him a year to start seeing the benefits of allowing others to lead in areas where he lacked training and experience. Today, his practice is stable and profitable because he has made the necessary management and financial changes.

The Hero is often the hardest physician to reach, but paradoxically, they also have the highest potential to change. When they finally open themselves to accept direction and consider the necessary tools, they can excel. Their confidence, once tempered with collaboration and humility, can drive success. These are the physicians who, once aligned with a good team, can dominate their field both in skill and business. They already believe in excellence, and with help, they can apply their desire for excellence to areas beyond patient care.

Strategies for the Hero

Strategic Delegation to Trusted Experts: The Hero thrives when surrounded by a high-performing team. Delegating key business functions, such as operations, billing, or marketing, to experienced professionals or a management services organization (MSO) allows the Hero to maintain focus on clinical excellence while ensuring the practice runs efficiently.

Data-Driven Decision Making: Appeal to the Hero's competitive nature by introducing objective performance metrics. Financial reports, patient outcome data, and operational benchmarks give them a measurable way to improve without feeling undermined.

Reframing Guidance as Strategic Partnership: Instead of presenting advice as correction, frame it as collaboration. The Hero is more receptive when solutions align with high performance, leadership, and mastery, rather than supervision.

Showcasing Peer Success Stories: Highlight case studies or testimonials from similarly skilled physicians who improved their practices by accepting business support. The knowledge of peers who succeed can validate change and reduce resistance to outside input.

Some Heroes may never be easy to work with, but it is possible to break through their initial wall of resistance. And behind that wall is often someone capable of achieving incredible success. It is easier to help a good doctor become a great business person than to turn a poor doctor into a good one.

Some individuals in healthcare may find themselves embodying a mix of both the Helper and the Hero qualities. These hybrid professionals often possess the altruistic drive of the Helper, with a deep sense of purpose and compassion for their patients, yet also carry the Hero's self-assurance and desire for excellence. By recognizing this balance, they can leverage the strengths of both categories. The Helper's commitment to patient care and their sense of moral obligation can be enriched by the Hero's confidence and leadership skills, creating a physician who not only provides exceptional care but also leads with strategic vision. On the other hand, the Hero's confidence and independence can be tempered with the Helper's humility and empathy, enabling them to approach business decisions with a more patient-centered mindset.

By incorporating elements from both perspectives, these individuals can build a medical practice that thrives on both compassionate care and sound business management, allowing them to excel in every aspect of their work without sacrificing their core values.

Chapter 4: Guilt
Feeling Bad for Making Money

As mentioned in the previous chapter, one of the most limiting factors in achieving success in the medical business is what I call the "Guilt of the Calling." This refers to a deeply ingrained societal perception that caring for someone, especially the sick or dying, should be a free service. There is a moral expectation that physicians should serve those in need without hesitation, and certainly without expectation of compensation. After all, how dare you ask for payment when their child is dying of cancer!

This mindset has become increasingly prevalent, particularly as the concept of access to healthcare as a right has gained traction in both public discourse and policy. The argument suggests that if freedom is a right without financial cost, then health and wellness should also be available without financial barriers. While noble in theory, this ideology places physicians in a no-win situation, pursuing a successful business risks being labeled greedy, while fulfilling their duty to care without compensation makes their practice unsustainable. The contradiction is stark: doctors are expected to serve, yet are vilified for seeking financial success.

Many began their career with a genuine sense of calling, a deep-seated drive to help others, especially those who are vulnerable or in need. That feeling is real, and I believe it can be harnessed to make us more empathetic, more compassionate providers. However, the conflict arises when trying to balance this calling with the realities of running a practice. Is it worse to lay off your staff because you provided care without payment, or to ask patients to take some financial responsibility for their own health? Expecting patients to contribute financially often leads to better compliance and healthier choices. Moreover, the more successful a provider becomes, the more resources they have to offer high-quality care to an even larger number of people.

I was fortunate to have learned this concept from great mentors early in my career. Thanks to the success of my practice, I've been able to lead and participate in mission trips to Mexico and Haiti, and to support care for the underserved in many other ways. If I let guilt about financial success take root, I would not have the means to support those efforts. My way of addressing the "Guilt of the Calling" is to provide the best care I can, and to not feel ashamed for valuing my time and expertise.

The stereotype of the rich doctor fuels this challenge. Yes, there was a time when physicians were well compensated. The caricature of the doctor with a country club membership, a luxury car, and a big house originated somewhere. That era has largely passed, and yet the perception is all too often distorted and weaponized.

This double standard is perpetuated by both the insurance industry and government agencies. Executives and policymakers enjoy lavish perks, cars, meals, and trips, all standard in their world of business. But if a physician were to receive the same, it would be considered unethical or exploitative. The message is clear: doctors can't be trusted with business incentives because they might prioritize their own interests over patient care.

But let me ask, has the insurance industry ever prioritized patient care over profit? Has any government-run agency been a shining example of efficient healthcare delivery? Physicians are held to the highest standards, both ethically and legally. If a doctor makes a poor choice, the consequences are swift: malpractice, loss of license, and even jail. Every product we use and every procedure we perform is judged based on patient outcomes.

This misconception is taken advantage of by those who run and regulate healthcare. How many times have you seen the finger pointed at the doctor as greedy and unconcerned? Why do things cost so much? Greedy Doctor! Why can't you get that medicine? Your doctor! Why can't the government fix healthcare? The Doctor! The manipulation of public perception is used to divert attention away from the real issues in healthcare. Follow the money, and you can easily see who makes and controls the decisions. Some examples of how the public can be swayed;

A patient came into my office after a recent joint replacement surgery. He had his itemized insurance bill in hand and opened the conversation with, "Well, Doctor, it must be nice to be you." I knew where this was headed, but asked anyway, "What do you mean?" He pulled open his billing paperwork and pointed to the total cost: $150,000. Now, a few things. First, he didn't have to pay that. His cost was a few thousand for the deductible. Second, what is billed and what is paid are not the same; however, that is another aspect of the problem and a topic for discussion. He was shocked by the cost, and he assumed I was pocketing the whole amount! So, I took the bill and pointed to the line that said "Physician Professional Fee: $2,400." "That is what I get paid," I calmly stated. At that point, he was truly surprised and shocked. He could not believe that was all I made for his surgery, especially in light of the total cost of the bill. Let's think about this! I spent almost a year getting to know him and trying conservative treatments for his joint pain and symptoms. Finally, we arrive at the point to proceed with surgery. I then performed a complex surgery with risks and complications that can occur. If anything happens during or after the surgery, or if the patient is not satisfied with the outcome, I risk being sued. I then have to follow this patient for years after the surgery, making sure it is functioning at a level he is happy with and has no issues in the years to come. All this for $2,400! I don't know of any other professional who would be called greedy for this. After I explained the bill, he shook my hand and said, "Doctor, you should get paid more!"

Another example illustrating the issue is that, more than twenty years ago, the insurance industry and the government analyzed population data and realized that the baby boomers were aging, which would cause a significant increase in future surgeries. In particular, it was noted that hip and knee replacements were predicted to increase in demand exponentially. This was going to cost them a large amount of money and lower profits. The answer? Since that time, they have decreased the payment for hip and knee replacements by 37–40 percent.[2] The surgery and risks haven't changed.

---

[2] Kim, Sunny. "Study Shows Increase of Hip And Knee Replacements in the US." Science Daily, April 14, 2008.

Hospital for Special Surgery. "Hip and Knee Replacements on the Rise." HSS.edu November 27, 2007.

Haglin, Jack M., et al. "Medicare Reimbursement for Hip and Knee Arthroplasty From 2000 to 2019: An Unsustainable Trend." PubMed, 2020.

Even with advances in technology and surgical technique, the basic elements of the procedure and care of the patient, before, during, and after the surgery, have not changed. However, I now earn that much less to do it. Try to name another product or service in which demand has increased approximately 14 percent per year to over 2.8 million cases per year, but the pay for that service has decreased by 40 percent.[3] For comparison, let's look at a real-world example of what a regular service business experienced. From 2020 to 2021, DoorDash's business increased 14–20 percent, with its revenue rising approximately 20 percent during the same period.[4] This shows the unique challenges that the business of medicine faces.

This manipulation of perception fosters guilt across our profession. We're told that medicine is a calling, and that helping people should be its own reward. This narrative discourages us from advocating for fair compensation. It trains both the public and providers to undervalue the most critical service in society. Think about it: isn't your healthcare the one thing worth paying the most for?

The irony is that when push comes to shove, people would give everything for a cure, for relief from pain, or the restoration of function. And yet they've been conditioned to expect it all for free, as a right, divorced from cost or value.

Haglin, Jack M., et al. Medicare Reimbursement for Primary and Revision Total Hip and Knee Arthroplasty: An Updated Analysis from 2000 to 2024." PubMed, 2025.

[3] Wiley-Blackwell. "Study Shows Increase of Hip and Knee Replacements in the US." Science Daily. www.sciencedaily.com/releases/2008/04/080414155247.htm (accessed May 17, 2025).

Kurtz S, Ong K, Lau E, Mowat F, Halpern M. Projections of primary and revision hip and knee arthroplasty in the United States from 2005 to 2030.

J Bone Joint Surg Am. 2007 Apr;89(4):780-785. doi: 10.2106/JBJS.F.00222. PMID: 17403800.

American Joint Replacement Registry (AJRR). (2023). 2023 Annual Report. American Academy of Orthopaedic Surgeons (AAOS).

[4] Statista. "Revenue of Leading Online Food Delivery Services in the United States from 2017 to 2021." Accessed August 13, 2025.

This mindset not only undervalues the provider but also sets up barriers to building a viable medical business. The guilt of the calling, coupled with distorted public opinion, limits what physicians can do. It distorts business strategies and stifles sustainability. Until we address this imbalance, we'll continue to see burnout, closures, and a decline in the very quality of care we all claim to value.

Chapter 5: The Choices You Can Make to Survive or Thrive

So with all the obstacles and challenges discussed throughout this book, what can the Medical Professional do? When it comes down to it, two main paths stand before you: the employment model or the self-employment option. Each comes with its own unique set of benefits and challenges, and understanding these deeply can help you make an informed decision that aligns with your personal and professional goals.

The Employment Model

This pathway has increasingly become the preferred option, especially for newly trained physicians entering the healthcare workforce. This trend is driven by several compelling factors that appeal to many practitioners, particularly those early in their careers.

One of the most attractive features of employment is paycheck security. The security of having a consistent, reliable income each month cannot be overstated. For many healthcare providers, especially those with student loans or family obligations, knowing that the funds will be available is a significant relief. This allows you to focus your energy where it truly matters, on patient care. Freed from the burdens of running a business, managing staff, or dealing with insurance claims, you can devote yourself fully to your medical practice.

The ability to concentrate on clinical work without the distractions of business management is a huge draw. You don't have to worry about hiring and firing decisions, payroll, rent, billing, or marketing. These tasks fall to someone else, and that provides a significant feeling of stress relief. You are paid for the hours you work or the patients you see, often with productivity bonuses; however, the financial risk is fundamentally limited.

Beyond the practicalities, there is also a psychological aspect at play. A recent survey found that having a sense of purpose in one's work was one of the leading motivators for the younger generation of physicians.[5] The employment model can help foster that sense of purpose, as your role is clearly defined: you are the provider, the caregiver, the expert. With a steady paycheck and fewer distractions, it can be easier to maintain job satisfaction.

However, this model is not without its drawbacks. One of the biggest concerns many providers express is the loss of autonomy. As an employee, you are not the decision-maker. You may find yourself having to comply with policies, schedules, or clinical protocols set by others, sometimes far removed from the realities of your daily practice. If you don't get along with a particular colleague or staff member, your ability to influence that dynamic may be limited. Need flexible hours or an extended vacation? Those might not be on the table.

Moreover, compensation in the employment model is often capped. Even if you go above and beyond, your pay is unlikely to increase significantly unless it is tied to specific productivity metrics or performance targets. These metrics can sometimes feel like arbitrary hurdles, emphasizing quantity of work over quality or patient-centered care. You may feel pressured to see more patients or rush appointments, which can detract from your professional satisfaction and ultimately impact patient outcomes.

The Self-Employment Option

This can vary widely, from solo practitioners managing their own small offices to large multi-specialty group practices with dozens of providers. While the diversity of practice structures means that experiences differ, some common themes unite self-employed physicians.

One of the biggest draws of self-employment is the control it offers. You are your boss, or at least a partner or decision-maker within your practice. This means you have significant influence over how you practice medicine and how your business is run. Want to implement a new treatment approach? You can do that. Want to customize office hours or take time off without asking permission? That's possible, too. The freedom to shape your

---

[5] Jackson Physician Search and LocumTenens.com. Is Medicine Still a Calling? Exploring Physician Attitudes About Purpose in Medicine. Alpharetta, GA: Jackson Physician Search, March 5, 2025.

practice in a way that matches your values and priorities is often described as incredibly empowering.

Income potential is another advantage. As an owner, you directly benefit from the success of your practice. If you build a strong patient base, add ancillary services, or develop new revenue streams, such as physical therapy or diagnostic testing, you can increase your earnings. Unlike employment, where pay is generally fixed or limited, self-employment offers the possibility of financial growth that aligns with your effort and business savvy.

But this model comes with significant responsibilities and risks. Running a practice means running a business. You must make or get help to make all business decisions, from hiring staff to negotiating with vendors, to handling insurance contracts and billing. You are responsible for ensuring the office operates smoothly and complies with all relevant regulations. You must handle the financial aspects, including paying bills, managing cash flow, and addressing unexpected expenses.

Patient care doesn't stop at the clinical interaction; you may also have to address patient complaints or disputes related to billing or scheduling. You may find yourself stretched thin between seeing patients and administrative duties. And when income fluctuates, whether due to changes in patient volume, reimbursement rates, or unexpected costs, your paycheck can shrink or disappear altogether. I have personally experienced periods where, for a month or multiple months, I took no paycheck home at all due to financial pressures in my practice.

Marketing and business development also fall on your shoulders. Growing your patient base might require outreach, advertising, or networking activities that don't come naturally to all physicians. This can be time-consuming and distracting from clinical work. Some find the entrepreneurial side exciting and fulfilling; others find it stressful and draining.

Both of these models come with pros and cons, and neither is inherently "better" than the other. The real deciding factor comes down to your goals, your personality, and what you value most in your professional life.

If your top priority is stability, predictability, and the ability to focus purely on clinical care without distractions, employment may be the best fit. If you value autonomy and control and have an appetite for business challenges and risk, self-employment can offer greater rewards, both financially and professionally.

Ask yourself: What factors matter most to you? Is it the security of a paycheck or the thrill of building something that is your own? Is it flexibility or predictability? What kind of work environment will help you thrive and deliver the highest quality patient care?

Remember, this is not a permanent decision. Many physicians move between these models at different points in their careers. Some start employed to gain experience and financial footing, and then transition to self-employment later. Others may find that employment suits them perfectly for their entire careers.

Ultimately, surviving and thriving in medicine means choosing a path that aligns with your values, ambitions, and lifestyle, one that enables you to deliver care in a manner that feels both meaningful and sustainable for you.

Chapter 6: Things That Give Me a Headache

The modern challenges in healthcare can be traced back to two fundamental issues: physicians have lost control of their profession, and patients no longer take responsibility for their health. While other factors certainly contribute to the difficulties of succeeding in the business of medicine, these two remain the most influential forces that have transformed healthcare in the United States.

In most industries, the person doing the work, the skilled expert, is at the heart of the business. The same principle should apply to medicine. Without the physician diagnosing illnesses, performing surgeries, or planning treatments, nothing happens. The provider should play a central role in approving medications, designing treatments, and establishing care standards tailored to each patient. They should also have a say in determining the cost and value of their time and expertise. After all, you expect this from your mechanic, contractor, or fitness coach, so why not from your doctor?

Unfortunately, money and power attract interference. Over time, other industries and interests have inserted themselves into healthcare, setting standards, approving treatments, and controlling payments. Physicians have been pushed to the bottom, no longer decision-makers but laborers. Much of this change has been driven by public perceptions shaped by the "rich doctor" stereotype and the moral expectations surrounding care. Doctors couldn't fight back without being labeled as greedy or unethical, so they didn't.

Yes, some of this was self-inflicted. Certain physicians did live up to the caricature, flaunting wealth, acting untouchable, and ignoring the warning signs. They assumed their central role in healthcare was secure. But once you lose control over how your service is delivered, how it's valued, and how it's reimbursed, you've lost more than your autonomy; you've lost your leverage.

Today, we see the consequences. Physicians are heavily restricted. We can't easily unionize or negotiate collectively. Declining poor insurance plans invite public outrage. You've probably seen it: a hospital or physician group stops accepting a particular insurer, and the news headlines scream about greedy doctors denying care. Social media follows with moral condemnation.

What's always forgotten in those moments is that physicians are human too. We spend a minimum of eleven years in training, four years of undergrad, four years of medical school, and at least three years in residency. Most of us graduate with over $200,000 in debt.[6] If we run our own practice, we also carry the responsibility of paying staff, covering building costs, and keeping the lights on. Yet somehow, we've become the least valued asset in the healthcare system.

And it's not just about money, it's about respect. If I were a patient, I would want my physician to be well-compensated and well-supported, so they could focus on providing the best possible care. Instead, we're expected to give everything and ask for nothing. Imagine if physicians nationwide stopped seeing patients or stopped accepting insurance altogether. You'd be furious. Outraged. "How dare they?" Yet, when airlines strike, teachers walk out, or contractors demand deposits up front, the public often sympathizes. Why the double standard?

As the movement grows to declare healthcare a "right," remember this: the people pushing for that right want to control it. And in that control, the provider, the only one who truly matters when it comes to your healthcare, is pushed further away from decision-making and the ability to provide quality care. It's time to start valuing physicians not as commodities, but as professionals whose expertise is irreplaceable.

The second core problem is the lack of patient accountability, both in terms of personal health and financial responsibility. Consider this analogy: most people know how to care for their car. If you burn out the tires or skip oil changes, you accept that breakdowns are a result of your actions. If the

---

[6] Association of American Medical Colleges. "You Can Afford Medical School." Last modified October 2024.

paint peels or the engine dies, it's on you to fix it and to pay for it.

But people don't treat their bodies with the same understanding. A diabetic with heart failure may drink energy drinks daily, binge on junk food, party on weekends, and then blame the doctor when we can't "fix" them. Or someone breaks their legs jumping off a cliff for social media content and is furious when told they may never walk normally again. The provider becomes the enemy for not performing a miracle. These patients demand cutting-edge procedures they find online, regardless of whether they are clinically appropriate or financially feasible.

This entitlement runs deep. Financially, too, many patients refuse responsibility. I've treated people with no insurance who crash expensive off-road vehicles, drive away in brand-new trucks, and refuse a payment plan for the surgeries that saved them. However, if you dare to suggest collections or upfront payment? That's viewed as unethical.

Why is it acceptable to spend on cigarettes, motorcycles, and luxury items, but not on your own healthcare? In what other industry would this be tolerated? Imagine walking into a restaurant, eating a full meal, and refusing to pay, only to receive sympathy for it. Yet that's what physicians face daily.

Of course, we do it anyway, because we care. However, over time, the weight of treating patients who refuse to take responsibility, either financially or medically, makes it emotionally exhausting and nearly impossible to sustain a successful business. And when the system bends under that pressure, some call for more government control or a single-payer model. We should not expect more oversight to fix these root problems. It doesn't restore physician control. It doesn't promote patient accountability. In fact, it often exacerbates both.

I understand, this may sound like a doctor just complaining about money. But that's only because you've been conditioned to see it that way. This isn't about greed. This is about sustainability. It's about recognizing the realities of the business of medicine and the unique challenges that limit success in this field.

The issues don't end with the loss of control and the absence of patient accountability. The pay physicians receive is also controlled by someone else. In fact, we don't set the rates we can charge or the reimbursement we receive for most of the services and procedures we provide. Imagine a business where you can't adjust your price to market demand or the complexity of the service performed. The doctor is truly at the mercy of insurance reimbursement and contracted payment.

One might ask, can't you bill the patient for the difference or negotiate with the insurance company for a higher reimbursement? Well, guess what? That has been severely limited, too. In most cases, for an insurance-covered procedure or service, it is illegal for the doctor to charge the patient more than the allowed amount. There are still some exceptions, but they are few and far between. Patients are conditioned to expect insurance to cover everything, and any additional charge is viewed negatively and often not paid.

The ability to negotiate with insurance companies has also been severely limited by recent legislation. In the past, doctors could provide out-of-network services, which allowed them to bill market rates when insurance reimbursement didn't match the cost of the service. This gave physicians some leverage, especially if they were one of the few performing a particular procedure or in high demand. Patients would put pressure on the insurance company to negotiate with the doctor. But in January 2022, the "No Surprises Act" was passed, eliminating out-of-network billing. It was sold as a protection for patients to avoid "surprise" bills, but in reality, it stripped physicians of their ability to negotiate with insurance companies and set their own rates.[7] For instance, I used to bill around $5,000 for a particular service when I was out-of-network, but after the bill was passed, I was paid $350 for the same case. My costs didn't change, yet all power and choice were taken away from the doctor and placed in the hands of insurance companies.

[7] Centers for Medicare & Medicaid Services. "No Surprises: Understand Your Rights Against Surprise Medical Bills." January 3, 2022.

U.S. Department of Labor. "Avoid Surprise Healthcare Expenses: How the No Surprises Act Can Protect You." Accessed May 18, 2025.

Like most businesses, healthcare is uniquely affected by rising costs. Employee wages and benefits, for example, are driven up by market competition and regulation, but physicians can't raise their prices to offset these increases. This forces practices to limit staff hours and availability, resulting in longer wait times for patients and increased pressure on providers. On top of that, physicians have to deal with malpractice insurance, which is a unique burden for those in the medical field. Litigation is pervasive in medicine, and malpractice lawsuits contribute significantly to the financial burden on practices.

Another significant barrier to success in healthcare is the compensation structure for providers. Each insurance carrier has its own rates for services and procedures, and physicians have almost no negotiating power. The only option is to refuse that insurance, which limits access for patients and, of course, puts the blame on the physicians. Some practices have chosen to take no or limited insurance, instead moving toward a concierge model. This model delivers more personalized care but at a direct cost to the patient. While I'm a fan of this model, it isn't easy to scale it for the general public. Most people can't afford the market value of care, and many are offended by the idea of paying for it directly.

Many doctors attempt to address these limitations by working harder, extending hours, staying open on weekends, and increasing the volume of patients they see. However, there are only so many hours in a day, and this approach can lead to burnout. The younger generation of healthcare providers is noticing the dissatisfaction among older providers and is increasingly opting for simpler employment models. They don't want to deal with the hassles of running a business. Instead, they prefer a steady paycheck and patient care without the burdens of ownership.

As the demands on physicians increase, they often work longer hours, which can result in burnout, stress, and a decline in their personal well-being.

Over 40 percent of physicians report feeling burnt out, and over 20 percent suffer from depression.[8] The pressures of this profession are taking a toll on their physical and emotional health. This cycle needs to change. The physician is the backbone of healthcare, and until they are given the respect, control, and compensation they deserve, the entire system will continue to falter.

[8] Fathi, Afshin, Saeid Sadeghieh Ahari, Firouz Amani, and Mohammad Reza Nikneghad. "Frequency of Hypertension and Obesity and Their Relationship with Lifestyle Factors (Nutritional Habits, Physical Activity, Cigarette Consumption) in Ardabil City Physicians, 2012–13." Indian Journal of Community Medicine 41, no. 4 (2016): 268–272.

Mata, Daniel A., M. A. Ramos, N. Bansal, R. Khan, C. Guille, E. Di Angelantonio, and S. Sen. "Prevalence of Depression and Depressive Symptoms Among Resident Physicians: A Systematic Review and Meta-analysis." JAMA 314, no. 22 (2015): 2373–2383.

Hughes, Patrick H., Nancy A. Brandenburg, David C. Baldwin Jr., Cheryl L. Storr, Kimberly M. Williams, John C. Anthony, and David V. Sheehan. "The Prevalence of Substance Use Disorders in American Physicians." Journal of Addiction Medicine 2, no. 4 (2008): 190–195.

Chapter 7: The Barriers Roadblocks and Stop Signs on Your Journey

There are hard barriers in the business of medicine that practitioners must face, and these barriers are often beyond individual control or influence. They represent the boundaries within which medical practices must operate, and they shape much of the environment in which healthcare providers deliver care. These barriers come in many forms, but some of the most significant are laws, regulations, insurance rules, and reimbursement structures. These elements serve as the invisible lines that define how medicine is practiced today.

Laws and regulations are perhaps the most rigid of these barriers. They establish the legal framework for medical practice, defining what can and cannot be done within it. For example, licensing requirements, privacy laws such as HIPAA, and standards for patient safety all create mandatory conditions that healthcare providers must follow. These rules exist to protect patients, ensure quality, and maintain ethical standards; however, they also create limitations. Changing these laws is not a simple task. It requires political advocacy, sustained efforts by professional organizations, and often years of negotiation and lobbying. For an individual provider or practice, the best approach is to clearly understand these legal boundaries and work efficiently within them, rather than attempting to push beyond or circumvent them on one's own.

Similarly, insurance companies and government payers impose their own set of restrictions through contracts and reimbursement policies. Insurance reimbursement is determined by complex agreements between payers and providers, which dictate the services covered and the corresponding rates. These contracts can be restrictive and often do not fully reflect the true cost or value of the care provided. Insurance companies may limit coverage for certain procedures or medications, impose prior authorization requirements, or deny claims based on technicalities. All of these factors create friction in the delivery of care and revenue collection. While there is some room to negotiate these contracts, especially for larger practices or groups with bargaining power, changes are slow and challenging to implement. Understanding the intricacies of these contracts and managing them effectively is crucial for a practice's financial health, but it requires specialized knowledge and effort.

Patient payments add another layer of complexity. Even when insurance covers a portion of the cost, patients are often responsible for co-pays, deductibles, and uncovered services. These payments are limited by several factors, including what insurance allows, what patients are willing or able to pay, and the overall market environment. There is a natural limit to how much a patient can or will pay out-of-pocket before it impacts their willingness or ability to seek care. This reality means that practices must carefully balance their pricing and collection policies with patient satisfaction and access to care. Cash or direct payments from patients, sometimes referred to as "self-pay," can be an essential revenue stream, particularly in areas or specialties where insurance coverage is limited or complex. However, building a practice model around direct patient payments requires a clear understanding of the patient population and market dynamics, as well as transparent communication about costs and payment expectations.

These barriers, legal, regulatory, insurance-related, and financial, outline the "box" within which providers must care for their patients. Knowing the edges of this box helps providers avoid frustration and wasted effort. Rather than attempting to remove these obstacles single-handedly, the goal is to navigate within the confines they create, finding pathways to efficiency and success without violating these essential rules. Recognizing the barriers also helps identify where advocacy and change are needed on a broader scale, and when it's worth investing time and resources to push for adjustments.

In many cases, working around or within these barriers means developing strategies that optimize existing resources, enhance operational efficiencies, and improve patient engagement and satisfaction. For example, better documentation and coding can maximize reimbursement within the constraints of insurance contracts. Transparent billing practices and patient education can help improve collections and reduce payment confusion. Leveraging technology, such as electronic health records and practice management systems, can streamline workflows to reduce administrative burden. All of these efforts are about adapting to the reality of these barriers, not trying to eliminate them outright.

Ultimately, the presence of these barriers is a defining feature of modern medical practice. They serve as guardrails that ensure care is delivered safely, fairly, and within established guidelines and protocols. While frustrating at times, they also create a framework that providers can learn to master. Success comes not from ignoring or resenting these barriers but from understanding their nature and limitations, then working creatively and persistently within them. This mindset allows providers to focus their energy on delivering high-quality care while maintaining a sustainable and compliant business operation. Recognizing the barriers for what they are, sometimes immovable, often challenging, but always present, is the first step toward building a resilient and effective medical practice.

THE BARRIERS
Roadblocks and Stop Signs on your journey

INSURANCE RESTRICTIONS

Coverage Limitations

Complex Contracts

LAWS & REGULATIONS

Established Legal Framework

Difficult to Change

FINANCIAL CONCERNS

Patient Payment Limits

Pricing & Collection Policies

Economic Environment

Part Two:
Foundations and Strategies

Chapter 8: Your Foundation
for Success
The Right Structure

When establishing a business, particularly in the healthcare industry, selecting the appropriate corporate structure is foundational. The right structure supports growth, ensures compliance, and mitigates legal and financial risks. Understanding long-term goals is the first step in structuring a business. Factors such as scalability, revenue streams, liability protection, and tax implications all play a role in determining the best path forward. For medical practices, state-specific regulations, such as the requirement in California for physicians to operate under professional corporations or individual S corporations, add another layer of complexity.

Several business structures exist, each with its own set of advantages and limitations. A sole proprietorship is the easiest to set up but offers no liability protection, making it a risky choice for medical professionals. A general partnership involves two or more individuals sharing business ownership, but partners also share liability, which may not be ideal in a high-risk field like healthcare. A professional corporation or S corporation, often required in states like California, provides pass-through taxation and limited liability but can complicate revenue distribution if not structured correctly. A limited liability company (LLC) offers liability protection with flexible tax treatment and is often utilized in healthcare as a Management Services Organization (MSO) to manage administrative functions, allowing physician-owned entities to focus on patient care. An MSO, typically structured as an LLC, oversees multiple business units, streamlining management of revenue streams and services while maintaining corporate protection and compliance.

Once the appropriate entity is selected, ensuring legal and tax compliance is the next critical step. Legal agreements, such as operating agreements for LLCs or shareholder agreements for corporations, must clearly define ownership, profit distribution, and decision-making processes. Physician groups should also establish contracts that address compensation models, non-compete clauses, and equity arrangements to ensure transparency and fairness.

Understanding tax implications is essential, as S corporations provide pass-through taxation but require strict IRS compliance, while LLCs offer tax flexibility but may be subject to self-employment taxes. Structuring your business properly can optimize tax benefits while ensuring adherence to healthcare laws.

With the legal foundation established, starting the business involves setting up financial systems such as business bank accounts, accounting, and payroll structures, as well as ensuring tax compliance. Healthcare businesses must adhere to regulations like HIPAA, the Stark Law, and the Anti-Kickback Statute, making regular legal audits essential.

Certain pitfalls must be avoided when structuring a business. Choosing the wrong entity type without considering future growth and tax implications can lead to costly restructuring. Inadequate legal agreements may result in partner disputes and compliance risks. Overlooking tax obligations can lead to penalties and audits, while failing to maintain corporate formalities, such as separating business and personal finances, can jeopardize liability protections.

Establishing the right business structure is a crucial decision that significantly impacts a company's growth, legal standing, and financial health. Whether forming a simple S corporation or a complex MSO, careful planning, legal consultation, and strategic foresight ensure a smoother path forward. Consulting with an experienced tax advisor and corporate attorney helps tailor the best structure for your specific needs, reducing future complications and enabling sustainable growth. Get the foundation right, and the next steps are less of a headache.

Key Takeaways

• *Choosing the right business structure is critical for long-term growth, compliance, and liability protection.*

- *Medical practices must consider state-specific laws, like California's requirement for professional corporations or S corporations.*

- *Management Services Organizations (MSOs), often structured as Limited Liability Companies (LLCs), are popular for separating administrative and clinical functions.*

- *Proper legal agreements and tax planning are essential to avoid future disputes and penalties.*

- *Mistakes such as poor entity choice, weak contracts, or tax non-compliance can threaten a business.*

YOUR FOUNDATION for SUCCESS: The Right Structure for You!

STRUCTURE	LIABILITY PROTECTION	TAX TREATMENT	BEST FOR
SOLE PROPRIETORSHIP	None	Personal Income Tax	Solo Practitioners
GENERAL PARTNERSHIP	Limited Liability shared among Partners	Personal Income Tax	Small Group Practice
S CORPORATION	Limited	Physician Owned Practice	Physician Owned Practice in State (like California)
PROFESSIONAL CORPORATION	Strong	Corporate: pass-through (S corp election)	Medical Practices requiring Special Licensing
LIMITED LIABILTY CORPORATION	Flexible	Flexible: Pass-through or Corporate	Medical Business ventures MUST maintain clear separation from Clinical Services

Chapter 9: Don't Do Things for Free
I Can't Be Any Clearer Than That

As a healthcare provider, you have spent years developing your skills and expertise. Your time is valuable, and yet many medical professionals often find themselves offering their services for free. This is not only unsustainable but also unfair to you and the entire healthcare system. It is time to change the mindset that physicians should offer their expertise at no cost. I hope to explain why you should never undervalue your time, the financial and ethical implications of working for free, and practical ways to ensure you are appropriately compensated for your services.

Medicine is often viewed as a noble profession, one in which providers are expected to be selfless and always available for their patients. This belief is deeply ingrained, often starting in medical school. The idea that doctors should prioritize care over compensation can lead to a sense of guilt when it comes to charging for services that may seem minor, such as reviewing test results over the phone or responding to emails.

However, this guilt is misplaced. No other profession expects highly trained professionals to work for free. Lawyers charge for consultations, accountants bill for their time, and even mechanics charge for diagnostic tests. So why should doctors be any different? The work you do, whether in the exam room or over the phone, has value and should be treated as such.

Every time you spend a few minutes answering a patient's email or reviewing a lab result over the phone, you are taking time away from other billable activities. This time adds up quickly, and if you were to calculate the revenue lost from unbilled services, the number would likely be staggering.

Furthermore, providing free services sets a precedent that your time is not worth compensation. Patients come to expect free advice, and once that expectation is established, it becomes difficult to change. Over time, this devalues not just your practice but the profession as a whole.

One argument against billing for every interaction is that it may inconvenience patients. However, scheduling a visit, whether in person or via telehealth, actually leads to better patient care. When a patient comes in for a scheduled appointment to review test results or discuss a condition, you can give them your full attention. This allows for a more thorough discussion, the opportunity to ask and answer questions, and a more personalized healthcare experience.

Quick phone calls and emails, on the other hand, often lead to misunderstandings or incomplete information. A patient may not fully grasp the significance of their lab results or may forget to ask important follow-up questions. By scheduling a visit, you ensure that all concerns are addressed comprehensively.

Consider this: If you spend an average of thirty minutes per day responding to emails or phone calls that are not billable, that adds up to two and a half hours per week. Over a year, this equates to 130 hours of unpaid work. If your hourly rate is $300, that is $39,000 in lost revenue annually. This is a conservative estimate; many providers spend far more time on unbilled services.

Beyond individual financial loss, offering free services also impacts the healthcare industry as a whole. When physicians routinely give away their expertise, it lowers the perceived value of medical care. Patients may come to expect free services and push back when they are charged for time and expertise, creating a ripple effect across the field.

To avoid providing patient care for free while still delivering excellent care, it is crucial to establish a structured system for handling patient inquiries. Not every patient question requires a doctor's response. Train medical assistants or nurses to handle routine inquiries. If the issue is more complex, then it can be escalated to a provider for a scheduled visit.

If a patient is unable to attend an in-person visit, schedule a telehealth appointment. Most insurance providers now reimburse for tele-health services, making this a viable option. However, if this current reimbursement model changes, then value your time and schedule an in-person visit. Patients should know that email and phone consultations are not free services. Have a policy in place and communicate it clearly to your patients. Use patient portals for minor questions and automated responses for frequently asked inquiries. This can help manage workload and ensure that only necessary consultations require direct physician involvement. Some insurance providers offer reimbursement for phone or email consultations. Make sure your billing department is aware of these opportunities, and then bill them appropriately.

Many providers worry about appearing greedy or unempathetic if they insist on billing for all services. However, this is a flawed perspective, and one that has unfortunately been ingrained into healthcare. Charging for your time does not mean you care any less about your patients. It allows you to provide better care because you are giving time and attention to that patient.

Patients expect to pay for professional services in every other industry. It is time for the medical field to align with this standard. You have spent years acquiring your knowledge, and it is only fair that you are compensated accordingly. Do not undervalue yourself, your expertise, or your time.

By establishing clear policies, leveraging technology, and adopting a mindset that values your expertise, you can create a practice that is both financially sustainable and patient-focused. Ultimately, knowing your worth and standing by it is not just good business; it's essential for delivering the best possible care to your patients.

Key Takeaways

• *Your Time is Valuable: Never undervalue your expertise by working for free. Every minute spent providing care should be compensated.*

• *Free Work Sets a Bad Precedent: Offering free services lowers the perceived value of your work and creates unrealistic patient expectations.*

• *Better Care Through Structured Appointments: Scheduling in-person or tele-health visits leads to better, more thorough patient care.*

- *Financial Impact is Significant: Unbilled time adds up quickly, leading to major financial losses over the year.*

- *Leverage Staff and Systems: Train medical assistants and nurses to handle simple patient questions and triage effectively.*

- *Clear Communication is Critical: Establish and explain your billing policies to patients upfront to avoid misunderstandings.*

- *Professional Standards Apply to Healthcare Too: Just like lawyers, accountants, and consultants, doctors should expect fair compensation for their time and expertise.*

EXAMPLE of FINANCIAL IMPACT

SCENARIO	ESTIMATED TIME LOST	REVENUE LOSS (at $300.- an hour)
30 min a day of Unpaid Work	2.5 hour a week	$750 a week
1 Year (52 weeks)	130 hours	$39,000 annually

HOW to MANAGE
PATIENT INQUIRES PROPERLY

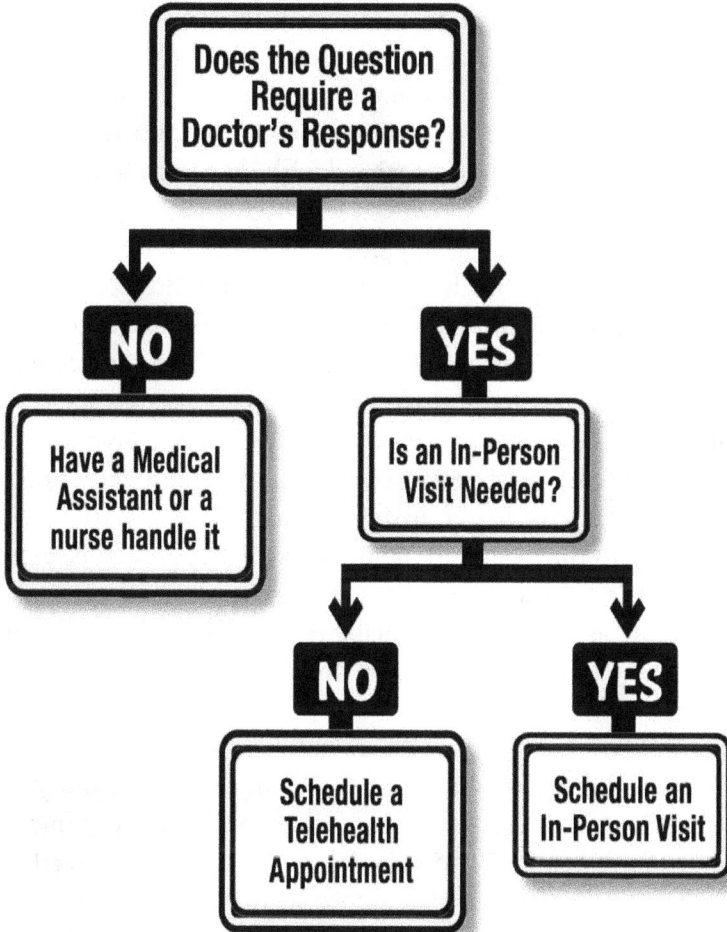

Does the Question Require a Doctor's Response?

NO

Have a Medical Assistant or a nurse handle it

YES

Is an In-Person Visit Needed?

NO

Schedule a Telehealth Appointment

YES

Schedule an In-Person Visit

Chapter 10: Ancillary Streams
Making Money that Flows to You

Developing a source of revenue that is in addition to or outside of your direct patient care can be a great way to improve your practice income. There are multiple ways to do this, and I will review a few. I recommend first exploring opportunities that directly relate to what you are already doing. This enables a smoother integration into your practice and minimizes the learning curve associated with introducing new services.

For example, if you routinely order urine drug tests in your practice, consider having your own lab system perform and interpret the tests. This will not only give you control over the testing but also quicker access to your patient results, thus improving patient care and satisfaction. When patients receive their test results faster, they experience less anxiety and uncertainty, which can enhance their overall trust in your practice. Additionally, you can bill for the lab services provided, creating an additional stream of revenue. You may start with basic toxicology screening and, as you grow comfortable with the regulatory requirements and operations, expand into other diagnostic lab tests. For instance, routine blood work, such as lipid panels, hemoglobin A1c tests for diabetes monitoring, or infection screening tests, can be integrated into your lab.

Of course, there are legal and regulatory laws and rules that have to be followed, and that is beyond the scope of this discussion, but you get my point. Ensuring compliance with CLIA (Clinical Laboratory Improvement Amendments) regulations and adhering to proper billing practices are essential when establishing any laboratory services. Working with a consultant who specializes in medical laboratory compliance can help navigate these complexities.

Another example is caring for patients with allergies. You could start to provide allergy testing and treatment within your practice. This can also be a new billable service you can offer. Skin prick testing or blood-based allergy testing can be conducted in-office with relatively low overhead. Once you have the testing capability in place, offering allergy immunotherapy in the form of subcutaneous (shots) or sublingual (drops) therapy could be another revenue source. Patients who suffer from seasonal allergies or chronic allergic reactions are often willing to pay for in-office solutions that save them time and provide relief.

If you provide bracing or splinting, you can start to provide some basic durable medical equipment (DME). Many patients require braces for orthopedic conditions, postoperative care, or chronic musculoskeletal conditions. Instead of sending them to an outside supplier, you can keep commonly used braces and splints in your office and dispense them directly. This not only provides a revenue stream but also enhances patient convenience. Patients appreciate being able to leave the office with everything they need, rather than having to make an additional stop at a medical supply store. Some practices have expanded into more specialized durable medical equipment (DME), such as custom orthotics, knee scooters, and portable TENS (transcutaneous electrical nerve stimulation) units for pain management. Non-prescription braces or supports can also be offered as a convenient option for patients. Many people need support braces for temporary injuries or chronic conditions, but may struggle to find the right one at a retail pharmacy. By offering these in-house, you can ensure they receive a quality product that fits properly and provides the necessary support. This can be expanded to include ergonomic supports, such as lumbar cushions for back pain, wrist braces for carpal tunnel syndrome, or compression sleeves for athletic injuries.

It is easier at first to start with services you already provide or problems you already treat. As your experience and success grow, you can expand to services outside your direct care. For example, if you frequently see patients who struggle with chronic pain, you might consider offering regenerative medicine treatments such as platelet-rich plasma (PRP) injections or stem cell therapy. These services are often cash-pay, which can help offset reimbursement challenges associated with traditional insurance-based medical care.

You can also grow into products that may benefit your patient population, such as vitamins or nutritional supplements tailored to your specialty.

For example, if you specialize in orthopedics, you might offer joint health supplements containing glucosamine, chondroitin, or collagen. If you are a dermatologist, you might offer medical-grade skincare products for acne, anti-aging, or hyperpigmentation. If you are a primary care physician managing a patient population with a high prevalence of metabolic disorders, consider providing medically supervised weight loss programs that include meal replacements and metabolic supplements.

Medications for pain or inflammation can also be a viable option. While prescription medications are subject to strict regulatory control, many over-the-counter (OTC) options can be provided directly to patients. Topical analgesics, anti-inflammatory creams, and natural pain relief options such as CBD-based products (where legally permitted) are becoming increasingly popular among patients seeking alternatives to traditional pharmaceuticals.

Wound healing and skin care products are another area where practices can develop additional revenue. If you treat patients with chronic wounds, post-surgical scars, or skin conditions, offering specialized wound dressings, silicone scar sheets, or advanced healing ointments can be beneficial. Patients trust their healthcare providers' recommendations over generic store-bought products, making this a valuable service to provide.

Depending on your practice scope and specialty, there may be many aspects that apply to your patients. The key is to assess the most common conditions you treat and determine what ancillary services or products can enhance patient outcomes while simultaneously generating additional income.

Another potential revenue stream is expanding telemedicine services. If you have expertise in a particular field, you can offer virtual consultations or second-opinion services. Many patients are willing to pay for direct access to an expert, particularly when facing complex medical issues that require specialized expertise.

Additionally, online education and content creation can be a lucrative option. If you frequently educate patients about specific medical conditions, you might consider creating digital courses, webinars, or e-books. Patients and other healthcare professionals often seek authoritative guidance, and providing these resources can establish your practice as a leader in your field while generating passive income.

Another approach is partnering with local businesses and gyms. If your practice focuses on sports medicine or rehabilitation, forming partnerships with fitness centers to provide injury screenings, movement assessments, or physical therapy sessions can be beneficial. Some practices even set up satellite clinics inside gyms, creating an additional revenue stream while increasing their visibility to an active patient base.

Offering concierge medical services is another way to enhance your income while improving patient satisfaction and overall well-being. In a concierge model, patients pay a membership fee for enhanced access to their physician. This could include longer appointment times, priority scheduling, wellness coaching, and personalized health plans tailored to individual needs. Many patients value the convenience and personalized attention that comes with concierge medicine, making it a viable option for physicians looking to transition away from traditional volume-based care.

Ultimately, offering these products or services will give your patients an improved sense of satisfaction as you give them choices and options for treatments. These also provide a way to help offset expenses and improve cash flow. The key is to start with what aligns most closely with your current practice, ensuring that any new service or product seamlessly integrates into your workflow. Over time, as you gain experience and understand patient demand, you can expand further into other revenue-generating opportunities. By diversifying your income sources, you can build a more financially stable and resilient practice while continuing to provide high-quality care to your patients.

Key Takeaways

• *Start with services related to what you already do to minimize the learning curve and ease integration.*

• *In-house lab testing (e.g., urine drug screens, blood work) enhances patient care and generates revenue.*

• *Offer allergy testing and treatment (skin prick, immunotherapy) within your practice.*

• *Provide basic DME (braces, splints) and expand to custom orthotics, TENS units, and ergonomic supports.*

• *Expand into cash-pay regenerative medicine (PRP injections, stem cell therapies).*

• *Sell specialty supplements or over-the-counter (OTC) products tailored to your patient base, such as those for joint health and skincare.*

• *Offer wound care and skin healing products to improve patient outcomes and loyalty.*

• *Develop telemedicine services for consultations or second opinions to widen reach.*

• *Create educational digital content (courses, webinars, e-books) for passive income.*

• *Partner with local gyms or businesses for referrals and satellite clinic opportunities.*

• *Consider a concierge medicine model for personalized, membership-based care.*

• *Focus on compliance (especially with labs and medications) to avoid legal risks.*

• *Start small, grow strategically based on patient needs and practice strengths.*

EXAMPLES of ANCILLARY REVENUE STREAMS

ANCILLARY STREAM	SERVICES / PRODUCTS	KEY BENEFITS
Lab Services	Urine Drug Test & Blood Panels	Faster Results & Billable Test
Allergy Services	Skin Testing & Innumotherapy	New Billing Opportunities
Durable Medical Equipment (DME)	Braces, Orthotics & TENS UntiS	Convenience for Patients & Extra Sales
Regenerative Medicine	PRP Injections & Stem Cell Therapy	Cash-Pay Income
Supplements & OTC Products	Joint Supplements, Skincare & Pain Relief Creams	Retail Revenue
Telemedicine	Virtual Consults & Second Opionions	Expanded Patient Base
Educational Content	Webinars, E-books & Online courses	Passive Income
Business Partnerships	Gym Injury Screens & Rehab Services	Increased Visibility & Referrals
Concierge Medicine	Personalized Care Plans & Priority Scheduling	Stable Membership Income

Chapter 11: Let's Make a Deal

One of the most significant areas of neglect I have observed in medical practices is the handling of insurance contracts. Most practices sign an initial contract with an insurance provider and never look back. In part, this is because reviewing contracts can be time-consuming, confusing, and complex. But at the end of the day, this is what determines how you get paid for doing your job. It is crucial to continually work towards securing appropriate reimbursement for the care you provide.

One of the first things to understand is that if you don't ask for better rates, you'll never get them. Insurance companies are never going to reach out and say, "We want to pay you more." They function as businesses, aiming to minimize their costs while maximizing their profits. Therefore, it falls on the healthcare provider to discuss and negotiate terms to ensure fair compensation. Many medical practices are unaware that most contracts can include a simple cost-of-living adjustment every few years. The surprising thing is that most practices don't even ask for this. Simply requesting a standard cost-of-living increase can lead to increased revenue for the same work. However, to truly maximize reimbursement and ensure that you are compensated fairly for the quality of care you provide, you need to take a proactive approach.

To add weight to your negotiations, you need data. Maintaining a simple database to track key metrics of your patient care can serve as a valuable tool. If you can demonstrate that your patient satisfaction rates or patient outcomes are higher than other practices in your area, you can justify an increase in your contracted reimbursement rates. For example, consider a practice that specializes in diabetes management. If that practice can show that its patients have better-controlled A1C levels, fewer adverse events, and overall better disease management compared to other providers in the area, that data becomes leverage in contract negotiations. Similarly, an orthopedic practice that can demonstrate lower complication rates, faster patient recovery times, and improved return-to-activity metrics can argue for higher reimbursement rates.

Consider an example like this. A mid-sized orthopedic practice in the Midwest realized that it had been operating under the same insurance contract for over a decade. The physicians noticed that their reimbursement rates had remained stagnant while their costs had increased. Upon reviewing their data, they found that their post-surgical complication rates were significantly lower than the national average, and their patients had an above-average return-to-activity rate within six months post-surgery. Armed with this data, they approached their primary insurance providers with a well-documented case for higher reimbursement. While the initial response from insurers was one of resistance, the practice persisted, citing comparative data from other providers in the region and demonstrating to the insurers that the high-quality care they delivered ultimately resulted in lower long-term costs for the insurance company. As a result, the practice was able to negotiate a fifteen percent increase in its contracted rates.

Insurance contracts can be complex, with multiple variables affecting reimbursement rates. Key factors that influence reimbursement include current Medicare rates, as many private insurance companies base their rates on a percentage of Medicare reimbursement. Understanding where your rates stand in comparison to Medicare can help you evaluate whether you're being paid fairly. Geographic adjustments also play a role, as different regions have different reimbursement rates based on cost-of-living and average medical costs. Quality metrics are becoming more influential as insurers increasingly tie reimbursement rates to quality outcomes rather than just the volume of services.

If the negotiation process seems confusing or intimidating, consider hiring professionals who specialize in handling insurance contract negotiations. One of the businesses I currently run focuses on this exact issue. However, not all contracting firms operate at the same level of expertise. Many will take the easiest route, making a simple call to request a cost-of-living increase, reporting back to the practice that they have increased contract rates, and collecting their fee. While this might provide some financial benefit, it leaves a significant amount of potential revenue on the table. A truly effective firm will go beyond the basic increase and work strategically to maximize contract terms. They will analyze your practice's performance data, compare it to industry benchmarks, and argue for meaningful reimbursement adjustments based on the quality of care you provide.

If you're looking to improve your reimbursement rates, there are several practical steps to take. Reviewing your current contracts is essential to understanding the details of your existing agreements, including reimbursement rates, renewal terms, and performance metrics. Collecting data by tracking key patient care metrics, such as patient satisfaction, treatment outcomes, and efficiency indicators, will give you a strong negotiating position. Benchmarking against competitors can provide additional insight into how your practice compares to others in your area or specialty. At a minimum, requesting a cost-of-living increase ensures that your contracts reflect inflation adjustments. If you choose to negotiate directly, building a compelling case with supporting data is crucial. If you decide to hire a negotiation expert, vetting them thoroughly will ensure they advocate for significant increases rather than just incremental adjustments.

Insurance contract negotiations are often overlooked in medical practices, but they play a crucial role in determining the financial health of a practice. Physicians and administrators should take a proactive approach, using data to strengthen their position and ensure they receive fair compensation for the quality care they provide. Whether you choose to handle negotiations in-house or hire a professional, the key takeaway is simple: if you don't ask, you won't receive. Make the effort, conduct the research, and secure reimbursement rates that accurately reflect the value of your services.

Key Takeaways

- *Neglecting insurance contracts is common.*

- *Most practices sign once and never renegotiate.*

- *Insurance companies won't offer better rates voluntarily.*

- *You must proactively ask and negotiate.*

- *Even small adjustments matter.*

- *Regularly requesting cost-of-living increases can boost revenue.*

- *Track patient outcomes, satisfaction, complication rates, recovery times, and other relevant metrics.*

- *Understand reimbursement factors, such as Medicare rates, geographic adjustments, and quality-based performance metrics.*

- *Some firms settle for minimal increases; great firms leverage their quality data for major gains.*

- *Review contracts regularly.*

- *Data is crucial for negotiations. Collect and organize performance data.*

- *Benchmark against competitors.*

- *Hiring help? Vet negotiation experts carefully.*

- *Ensure they aim for substantial improvements, not just quick wins.*

- *If you don't ask, you won't receive. Take control of your financial future.*

CONTRACTING STRATEGIES

ACTION	IMPACT
Review Existing Insurance Contracts	Identify outdated rates & unfavorable terms
Request cost-of-living Adjustments	Achieve immediate revenue increases with minimal effort
Collect & Track Performance Data	Build strong, evidence-based cases for higher reimbursements
Benchmark Against Competitors	Strengthen negotiation position by showing comparative advatages
Negotiate Proactively with Insurers	Secure better contract terms & higher pay rates
Hire & Vet Expert Negotiators	Maximize contract improvements beyond basic inflation adjustments
Understand Medicare & Regional Rates	Evaluate if you are being paid fairly

Chapter 12: Creating Businesses Creates Opportunities

Similar to ancillary streams, side businesses can be a significant source of revenue. In reality, they are a more formal extension of ancillary revenue streams. The key is to identify opportunities that closely align with your practice, leveraging services you already use and trust. For example, in my practice, we noticed that we were referring a large number of patients to chiropractic services. Instead of sending that revenue elsewhere, we decided to open our own chiropractic business. Of course, there are specific rules and legal requirements that must be followed carefully when expanding in this way, but with proper planning and compliance, it is entirely possible.

By integrating these services within our practice, we not only ensured better continuity of care for our patients but also created an additional revenue stream that we could control. It made sense, because we were already sending our patients to these services, we simply brought them in-house. This enhanced both the patient experience and our business sustainability.

Encouraged by this success, we expanded further and opened a full-service laboratory. This required additional work, certification, and adherence to regulatory guidelines, but once established, it became an invaluable part of our practice. Again, we were already using laboratory services routinely, so by taking control of this aspect, we reaped direct financial benefits from something that was already an integral part of patient care.

Expanding beyond direct patient services, we also launched a revenue cycle management company. This business initially started as a solution for our own billing, coding, and contract negotiation issues. Like all medical practices, we require these essential services to function efficiently. Once we established a well-run system for ourselves, we recognized that other practices could benefit from the same expertise, and so we scaled the business into a stand-alone company serving external clients. This allowed us to transform a necessary expense into a profit center, reducing costs for our practice while generating revenue by providing these services to others.

While some of these business ventures may seem like large, difficult tasks, and you may be wondering how you could ever find the time to pursue them, the real question you should be asking is: Can you afford not to? Yes, there is a learning curve, and you will face challenges along the way. However, the reward of generating additional income from services you are already using makes the effort worthwhile. The key is to start with something simple and familiar.

For example, one practice decided to start selling health-related products. These were products they were already recommending to their patients, nutritional supplements, orthopedic supports, and wellness items. Instead of sending patients to third-party retailers, they sourced the products they believed in, branded them with their private label, and offered them directly to their patients. Not only did this create an additional revenue stream, but it also allowed them to ensure their patients were using high-quality, trusted products.

Expanding your practice into side businesses does not necessarily mean opening large-scale operations immediately. The best way to begin is by looking at the services you already use and considering how you can integrate them into your business model. Many physicians and practice owners overlook opportunities that are right in front of them simply because they are accustomed to referring patients elsewhere. Whether it is diagnostic services, therapy, nutritional products, or even patient education resources, many potential business expansions are natural extensions of the care you already provide.

One critical aspect of developing side businesses is ensuring compliance with all regulatory and legal requirements. Depending on your area of specialization and the nature of the services you are considering, there may be licensing, accreditation, and operational guidelines to follow. This is particularly important in healthcare-related businesses, where patient care and ethical considerations must always come first. However, these hurdles should not deter you. With careful planning and consultation with legal and regulatory experts, you can successfully navigate these complexities.

Beyond compliance, it is essential to consider the operational structure of your side business. Will it be managed within your existing practice, or will it function as a separate entity? Some businesses, such as a laboratory or therapy center, may be best operated as subsidiaries of the main practice, while others, like a revenue management company, could function as an entirely independent business. Each approach has its advantages and should be tailored to the specific needs and goals of your practice.

Marketing and patient education are also critical components of successfully integrating a side business. Patients need to be informed about the availability of these services and why they benefit from utilizing them through your practice rather than seeking them elsewhere. Transparency and trust are key; if patients understand that they are receiving high-quality, convenient, and competitively priced services, they will be more likely to take advantage of them. This applies to everything from laboratory testing, therapy services, to health-related retail products.

Another example of a simple yet effective side business is in-office dispensing of medications. Many physicians hesitate to enter this space, assuming it is too complex or heavily regulated. However, with the right setup, offering commonly prescribed medications within your practice can enhance patient convenience while also generating revenue. Patients appreciate the ability to receive necessary medications immediately rather than making an additional trip to the pharmacy. Again, this is an example of leveraging something your practice already does, prescribing medication, and transforming it into a more seamless, integrated service.

As you explore different side business opportunities, it is crucial to balance growth with sustainability. Expanding too quickly or without proper planning can create operational inefficiencies and divert attention from patient care. Instead, a measured approach, starting with small, manageable additions and scaling as you gain experience, tends to yield the best results. Many successful practices that have ventured into side businesses started with one additional service, and gradually expanded as they refined their processes and confirmed the financial viability of their model.

Ultimately, the goal is to align these business ventures with your practice's core mission: providing high-quality patient care. Side businesses should enhance, not detract from, the patient experience. When executed correctly, they not only improve financial stability but also contribute to better patient outcomes by offering more comprehensive, convenient, and accessible services. The key is to recognize that you are already engaging with many of these services in some capacity. Rather than sending patients elsewhere, consider how you can bring these offerings into your practice in a way that benefits both your patients and your bottom line.

There is no single right way to expand into side businesses, and each practice will have unique opportunities based on its specialty, patient population, and market conditions. The important thing is to remain open to new possibilities and approach them with a strategic mindset. Every additional revenue stream you develop strengthens your practice's financial foundation, providing greater security and flexibility in an ever-changing healthcare landscape. The most successful practice owners are those who recognize opportunities, take calculated risks, and leverage their existing expertise to build businesses that support both their patients and their professional growth.

Key Takeaways

- *Side Businesses = Formal Ancillary Revenue.*
Expand services closely related to your practice to generate new income.

- *Leverage Existing Patient Needs: Identify services you already refer out (e.g., chiropractic care, laboratory services) and bring them in-house to enhance your capabilities and improve patient care.*

- *Start Simple and Familiar: Begin with services or products you already recommend (e.g., supplements, orthopedic supports).*

- *Decide on Operational Structure: Choose between integrating services into your practice or creating separate entities.*

- *Educate and Inform Patients: Transparent marketing fosters trust and encourages patients to adopt new services.*

- *Scale Carefully: Expand gradually to avoid operational inefficiencies and maintain optimal patient care.*

- *Align with Core Mission: Side businesses should enhance patient experience, not compromise it.*

- *Strategic Mindset is Critical: Recognize opportunities, take calculated risks, and leverage your strengths.*

OPPORTUNITIES

OPPORTUNITY TYPE	EXAMPLE SERVICE	KEY BENEFITS
Patient Care Extensions	Chiropractic & Physical Therapy	Improve continuity & convenience
Diagnostics & Testing	Laboratory & Imaging	Control quality & create new revenue
Practice Operations	Revenue Cycle Management (RCM)	Turn expenses into profit
Patient Convenience	In-office Medication Dispensing	Enhance service & revenue
Health & Wellness Products	Supplements, Braces & Health Goods	Provide trusted private-label options

Chapter 13: Your Opinion, Expertise, and Time Are Worth a Lot

As a healthcare provider, your expertise and knowledge are valuable assets that can significantly contribute to your financial and professional growth. There are numerous ways to supplement your income by utilizing your skills and experience, and consulting is one of the most lucrative and fulfilling options. While it requires setting aside time from your primary practice, the rewards can be substantial.

One of the most well-known and rewarding consulting roles for physicians is serving as a medical expert in legal cases. Attorneys often hire physicians to serve as expert witnesses or to provide professional opinions on various legal matters. The demand for medical expertise in the legal field spans cases involving medical malpractice, personal injury, workers' compensation, disability claims, and even criminal proceedings. As an expert witness, you may be called upon to review medical records, provide written opinions, and testify in depositions or court. The ability to clearly articulate medical facts and opinions is essential in this role. Depending on your specialty and experience, you can charge substantial fees for your time. Some physicians earn hundreds of dollars per hour as expert witnesses.

For example, an orthopedic surgeon might review a case in which a patient claims a surgical procedure was performed incorrectly, resulting in long-term disability. The surgeon would review medical records, provide an opinion on whether the standard of care was met, and potentially testify in court regarding their findings. Similarly, a neurologist might be called upon to assess a case involving traumatic brain injury from a car accident, determining whether the symptoms align with the reported mechanism of injury.

For those who prefer to stay out of the courtroom, independent case reviews provide an alternative avenue for consulting. These involve evaluating medical records and treatment decisions to determine if the standard of care was met. Attorneys rely on these reviews to decide whether a case is worth pursuing or to prepare for litigation. For instance, a physician might be asked to review the treatment of a patient who suffered complications after surgery. The attorney may want an unbiased medical opinion to determine whether the surgeon followed proper protocols or if there was negligence involved. This type of consulting work can be done remotely, making it a convenient option for busy physicians.

Another profitable consulting opportunity is conducting Independent Medical Examinations (IMEs). IMEs are frequently utilized in workers' compensation cases, personal injury claims, and disability assessments. Insurance companies, employers, and attorneys engage independent providers to evaluate injured individuals, determine the severity of their injuries, and assess whether they have achieved maximum medical improvement.

For example, a physician may be asked to examine a construction worker who suffered a back injury on the job. The physician would assess the severity of the injury, determine if the worker is capable of returning to work, and provide recommendations for further treatment or permanent disability ratings. IMEs can be conducted within your current practice or as a separate consulting business. Some physicians perform IMEs on weekends or set aside specific days in their schedule for this type of work. The compensation for IMEs can be substantial, with fees ranging from a few hundred to several thousand dollars per evaluation, depending on the case's complexity and the physician's expertise.

Physicians are valuable resources for medical device companies and pharmaceutical firms, providing insights into product development, clinical applications, and marketing strategies. Consulting for these industries can take several forms, including product development, clinical trials, and educational roles. Medical device manufacturers often seek input from physicians during the development of new products. This can include evaluating prototypes, providing feedback on usability, and participating in clinical trials to assess safety and efficacy. Physicians can also contribute to the design of surgical instruments and the development of procedural techniques. For instance, an orthopedic surgeon might work with a company developing a new type of knee implant. The surgeon would test the device in a simulated surgical setting, provide feedback on its design, and suggest modifications to improve functionality.

In some cases, physicians may be invited to serve as key opinion leaders, helping to promote new products within the medical community. Pharmaceutical companies frequently conduct clinical trials to evaluate new drugs and treatments. Physicians can participate by enrolling patients, collecting data, and analyzing outcomes. This not only provides an additional revenue stream but also allows physicians to stay at the forefront of medical advancements.

During the COVID-19 pandemic, many physicians participated in clinical trials for experimental treatments and vaccines. This not only helped advance medical research but also provided financial support for their practices during a challenging time. Physicians involved in clinical trials can receive compensation for their time and effort, as well as funding for research-related expenses.

Another consulting opportunity in the medical device and pharmaceutical industries is serving as a speaker or educator. Companies often seek experienced clinicians to present at conferences, lead training sessions, or provide continuing medical education courses. For example, a cardiologist with expertise in interventional procedures might be invited to give a presentation on the latest advancements in stent technology. A neurologist specializing in migraine treatment might lead a workshop on new pharmaceutical therapies. These engagements can be highly rewarding, both financially and professionally, allowing providers to share their knowledge while expanding their networks.

For those interested in teaching, becoming a medical preceptor for students or residents is another opportunity to generate additional income. As a preceptor, you guide medical students, interns, or residents through their clinical rotations, offering real-world insight into patient care. Not only is this a fulfilling way to contribute to the future of the medical profession, but it can also be financially rewarding. Preceptors often receive compensation for their time, and the experience can enhance your leadership and mentorship skills.

If you're interested in pursuing consulting opportunities, the first step is to evaluate your expertise and interests. Consider what areas of expertise you can offer and what type of consulting work aligns with your schedule and professional goals. Networking is key to securing consulting opportunities. Start by reaching out to colleagues who have experience in consulting, joining professional organizations, and attending industry conferences. Many consulting opportunities arise through word-of-mouth referrals, so establishing a strong professional reputation is essential.

When pursuing consulting opportunities, the most essential factor to consider is the amount of time required. Time is the one resource you can never get back, so it's vital to evaluate whether the time investment is worth the return. Too often, professionals overlook the time needed to fulfill a consulting role, focusing primarily on the potential financial gain. However, it's vital to consider whether the time spent will allow for personal balance and won't detract from patient care, family, or personal health. While consulting can be highly lucrative, opportunities that demand excessive time and energy may not be worth it, especially if they cause burnout or compromise the quality of your primary practice. The most valuable consulting opportunities will align with your current work schedule, create passive income, or integrate seamlessly with your existing responsibilities. Passive income, such as royalties, investments, or digital products, enables ongoing income generation with minimal effort after the initial setup. These types of opportunities offer a high return on your time investment.

While consulting can be lucrative, it's crucial to balance it with your primary practice. Establish clear boundaries to prevent consulting work from interfering with patient care or leading to burnout. Many physicians dedicate specific days or evenings to consulting activities to maintain a healthy work–life balance. Ultimately, the most successful professionals understand that time is a non-renewable asset. Instead of trading more hours for money, the goal is to leverage expertise and create income streams that enhance both your professional and personal life.

Key Takeaways

- *Consulting is a valuable way for physicians to supplement their income, but it requires extra time and effort.*

• *Medical expert work is highly sought after in legal cases, involving record review, written opinions, depositions, and court testimony.*

• *Independent case reviews offer a way to consult without appearing in court, providing unbiased medical opinions remotely.*

• *Independent Medical Examinations (IMEs) are lucrative opportunities to assess injuries for legal and insurance purposes, often done alongside regular practice.*

• *Consulting with medical device and pharmaceutical companies can involve product development, clinical trials, and educational activities.*

• *Speaking and educational roles within companies enable physicians to share their expertise while expanding their professional networks.*

• *Networking and building a strong professional reputation are essential for securing consulting opportunities.*

• *Maintaining work–life balance is crucial to prevent consulting work from interfering with patient care or causing burnout.*

• *Time is your most valuable and non-renewable asset; always factor it heavily when evaluating income opportunities.*

• *Balance opportunity cost, ensure new ventures don't detract too much from primary work, family, or personal interests.*

• *Recognize and charge appropriately for your time; healthcare providers often undervalue their time compared to other high-level professionals.*

• *It's never too late to start. Begin by exploring income streams that align with your skills and priorities at any stage in your career.*

VALUE YOUR TIME: KEY TAKEAWAYS

Time is your most valuable and non-renewable asset. Always factor it heavily when evaluating income opportunities

Assess the return on time investment. Prioritize opportunities that provide significant value for the time required.

Be wary of "lucrative" ventures that demand excessive labor, stress, or time away from other priorities.

Focus on revenue streams that integrate with existing work. Create passive income, or enhance current services.

Passive income is crucial. Aim for opportunities that generate earnings with minimal ongoing effort.

Leverage current expertise. Build income streams based on skills and services you already provide

It is never too late to start. Begin exploring income streams that align with your skills and priorities at any stage in your career.

Evaluate scalability. Prioritize opportunities that can grow without consuming more of your time.

Balance opportunity cost. Ensure new ventures do not detract too much from primary work, family, or personal time.

SUMMARY of CONSULTING OPPORTUNITIES for PHYSICIANS

CONSULTING TYPE	DESCRIPTION	TYPICAL ACTIVITIES	POTENTIAL INCOME
Medical Expert in Legal Cases	Physician provides Expert Opinions & Testimony	Case review, written opinions & depositions	$300.00 - $800.00 an hour
Independent Case Reviews	Remote Review of Cases	Evaluate records, write reports & provide opinions	$200.00 - $500.00 an hour
Independent Medical Examinations	Evaluate patient injuries to determine appropriate care	Physical exams, records review & written reports	$200.00 - $500.00 an hour
Medical Device Consulting	Participate in or Develop Clinical Trails	Enroll patients, collecting data, analyze results & lead educational sessions	$150.00 - $400.00 an hour
Pharmaceutical Consulting	Share Clinical Expertise through Lectures, Panels & CME events	Present at conferences, lead workshops & serve on advisory boards.	$200.00 - $400.00 an hour
Speaking & Educational Engagements	Share Clinical Expertise through Lectures, Panels & CME events.	Build visibility through publications, social media & CME forums	$1,000.00 - $10,000.00 per event (varies widely)

Chapter 14: Playing with the Big Boys

There can be significant opportunities in forming aligned partnerships with hospitals or health systems. Many health systems have cost-saving programs that share a portion of those savings with healthcare providers. These programs often focus on efficiency improvements, waste reduction, and optimized supply chain management. While participation in these programs can be beneficial, the shared revenue for providers is typically modest. In my experience, these programs rarely result in substantial increases in overall income. The bureaucratic nature of large health systems, coupled with complex formulas used to determine savings distribution, often leaves providers receiving a fraction of what they may have expected. The administrative burden and required compliance can also offset the financial benefits.

Beyond cost-saving programs, more substantial opportunities exist through shared ownership arrangements in clinics or surgical centers. Many hospital systems actively seek partnerships with providers or groups to expand their footprint and improve service delivery. This might involve joint ventures where both parties invest in building new facilities, such as outpatient clinics or specialty care centers. These partnerships allow providers to share the costs and risks associated with expansion while benefiting from the hospital system's established infrastructure. The system's existing relationships with payers and vendors can streamline operations, making it easier to navigate the regulatory environment, obtain necessary certifications, and establish payer contracts.

One particularly attractive opportunity is co-ownership in an ambulatory surgical or procedural center. As healthcare increasingly shifts toward outpatient settings, hospitals recognize the financial and operational advantages of these facilities. Partnering with a hospital system in such a venture can provide significant benefits, including access to capital, reduced startup risk, and integration into a larger referral network. The system may assist with obtaining accreditation, managing supply chain logistics, and negotiating more favorable reimbursement rates. In return, providers benefit from increased efficiency, reduced overhead costs, and enhanced patient access. However, these partnerships require careful structuring to ensure equitable profit-sharing and long-term alignment of interests. If the health system retains too much control, providers may find themselves in a subservient position, limiting their autonomy in decision-making.

Another avenue for collaboration is through practice expansion. Many hospital systems actively support the growth of independent practices by assisting with provider recruitment and offering financial incentives to encourage this growth. For example, a hospital system may provide income guarantees for new hires, covering a portion of their salary during the initial ramp-up period. This can be particularly valuable for practices looking to expand into new geographic areas or add subspecialties. In some cases, the health system may also contribute to marketing and operational costs, reducing the financial burden on the practice. These arrangements can accelerate growth and increase patient volume, but they also require careful negotiation. If not structured properly, they can lead to an over-reliance on the hospital system, making it difficult to maintain independence.

Despite the potential benefits, there are inherent risks in partnering with hospital systems. While these organizations may present themselves as collaborative partners, their primary obligation is to their own financial stability and institutional goals. Leadership changes, budget cuts, or strategic realignments can quickly alter the nature of a partnership, leaving providers in precarious positions. A hospital system that once championed physician-led initiatives may suddenly shift priorities, cutting funding or restructuring agreements in ways that disadvantage independent providers. It is not uncommon for hospitals to buy out physician-owned shares in joint ventures, often at less favorable terms than initially promised. In such cases, physicians may find themselves pushed out of leadership roles, losing both financial and operational control.

An example of this dynamic can be seen in the proliferation of hospital-employed physician networks. Many providers initially join these networks under the promise of administrative support, stable salaries, and reduced operational burdens. However, once they become employees of the system, they may lose autonomy over clinical decisions, scheduling, and even patient referrals. Some hospitals implement restrictive covenants or non-compete clauses that make it difficult for providers to leave and practice independently. If the hospital decides to restructure or consolidate services, employed providers may find themselves reassigned, forced into new roles, or even terminated. These risks highlight the importance of maintaining a degree of independence, even when entering into seemingly beneficial agreements.

Numerous examples of misaligned incentives and conflicts of interest mark the history of physician-hospital partnerships. One well-documented case involved a group of orthopedic surgeons who partnered with a hospital system to develop a specialty surgical center. Initially, the arrangement was highly profitable, with both parties benefiting from increased procedural volume and efficiency. However, after several years, the hospital system decided to expand its outpatient surgery division, creating direct competition. Using its financial resources and payer leverage, the system began shifting referrals away from the physician-owned center, ultimately forcing the surgeons to sell their shares at a loss. This type of scenario is not uncommon and underscores the need for providers to maintain a contingency plan when engaging in hospital partnerships.

Another example can be found in the realm of accountable care organizations (ACOs) and value-based care arrangements. Many hospital systems encourage providers to participate in these models, promising shared savings and enhanced care coordination. While the concept is appealing, the financial benefits often fail to materialize as expected. The majority of savings in these programs tend to be absorbed by the hospital system, leaving individual providers with minimal financial upside. Additionally, the reporting requirements and quality metrics imposed by ACOs can be burdensome, requiring significant administrative effort with little direct compensation. Providers who enter these arrangements without a clear understanding of the financial structure may find themselves doing more work for less reimbursement.

Given these challenges, providers must approach hospital partnerships with a strategic mindset. Due diligence is essential when evaluating any potential agreement. Legal and financial advisors should be involved in contract negotiations to ensure that terms are fair and protect the provider's long-term interests. Providers should also strive to maintain some degree of control in joint ventures, whether through board representation, defined exit strategies, or contractual safeguards that protect against unilateral changes by the hospital system. Establishing a diversified revenue stream, such as maintaining independent practice operations alongside hospital-affiliated ventures, can also mitigate risk.

Ultimately, partnerships with hospitals and health systems can be valuable when structured correctly. They offer opportunities for growth, shared investment, and enhanced patient care. However, providers must remain vigilant and skeptical, recognizing that hospital systems prioritize their institutional survival above all else. Entering these partnerships with clear expectations, strong contractual protections, and an independent mindset can help ensure that the benefits outweigh the risks. While collaboration can be productive, blind trust in the system is a mistake. Providers should engage with health systems as strategic partners, not as dependents, maintaining leverage and autonomy wherever possible.

Key Takeaways:

• *Hospital partnerships offer opportunities through cost-saving programs, shared ownership in facilities, and practice expansion support.*

• *Cost-saving programs often yield modest provider income due to complex distribution formulas and high administrative burdens.*

• *Shared ownership in clinics or ambulatory surgical centers can be lucrative, but it must be carefully structured to protect provider autonomy and ensure fair profit-sharing.*

• *Practice expansion deals (e.g., recruitment help, income guarantees) can accelerate growth but may risk over-dependence on hospital systems.*

• *Risks of hospital partnerships include leadership changes, buyouts, loss of clinical autonomy, and unfavorable restructuring.*

• *Employed physician models can restrict provider autonomy through non-compete agreements, forced role changes, and limited control over patient care.*

• *ACO and value-based care arrangements often overpromise and underdeliver financial rewards while adding administrative burden.*

• *Due diligence is critical: Involve legal and financial advisors, insist on clear terms, and build in protections and exit strategies.*

• *Maintain independence whenever possible by diversifying revenue streams and negotiating for governance rights in joint ventures. A strategic mindset over blind trust is essential when engaging with hospital systems.*

PLAYING with the BIG BOYS

OPPORTUNITIES

Hospital partnerships offer opportunities through cost-saving programs, shared ownership in facilities, and practice expansion support.

LIMITATIONS

Cost-saving programs usually result in modest provider income due to complex distribution formulas and high administrative burdens

RISKS

Risks of hospital partnerships include leadership changes, buyouts, loss of clinical autonomy, and unfavorable restructuring.

KEY STRATEGIES

Due diligence is critical: involve legal and financial advisors, insist on clear terms, and build in protections and exit strategies.

Chapter 15: The New World Ahead

The future of healthcare presents a unique set of challenges and opportunities, many of which are shaped by the rapid evolution of technology and a shifting healthcare landscape. As the industry continues to evolve, many providers, especially those with years of experience, find themselves reflecting on a time when medicine felt more personal, with lighter administrative burdens and stronger doctor–patient relationships. These physicians often reminisce about when they had more autonomy, fairer reimbursements, and fewer regulations. However, they also express frustration over increasing consolidation, rising costs, and mounting regulations that threaten their independence and ability to practice medicine as they once did. As the profession transforms, some providers may choose to retire, others may leave the field, and some practices may close. However, for those willing to adapt, embrace change, and explore new opportunities, the future of healthcare still holds significant promise.

A major shift occurring in healthcare is the transition from fee-for-service to value-based care. This change emphasizes efficiency, quality, and patient outcomes rather than volume. While it requires investment in data analytics and care coordination, practices that successfully integrate these principles stand to benefit from incentives, improved contracts with payers, and increased patient satisfaction. In this new model, the focus on preventive care, chronic disease management, and a holistic approach to healthcare aligns with patient expectations.

Technology plays a pivotal role in reshaping healthcare practices. Telemedicine, artificial intelligence, remote patient monitoring, and digital health tools are transforming the way healthcare providers interact with patients and manage care. Telemedicine has proven invaluable for reaching patients in remote areas, reducing unnecessary office visits, and providing convenient follow-ups. Similarly, remote patient monitoring allows for real-time tracking of chronic conditions, reducing hospital admissions and improving outcomes. AI is helping streamline administrative tasks, enhance diagnostics, and support clinical decision-making. Providers who embrace these technologies rather than resist them will not only enhance their efficiency and expand their patient base but will also improve the quality of care they provide.

The continued advancement of AI, particularly in machine learning and natural language processing, has led to the development of powerful tools that can improve medical practice. AI-driven medical scribing platforms are revolutionizing documentation by enabling real-time transcription of patient encounters. These tools capture every detail of a visit, ensuring the process is accurate, HIPAA-compliant, and seamlessly integrated into electronic health records (EHRs). This reduces the burden of documentation, which has long been a source of stress and burnout for healthcare providers, allowing them to engage more deeply with patients and improve the overall patient experience. AI-enhanced scribing not only boosts efficiency but also ensures more consistent and accurate documentation, particularly in specialties where precise record-keeping is critical, such as cardiology, oncology, and orthopedics.

Beyond documentation, AI is also transforming billing and coding. Traditional methods of manual coding often lead to inefficiencies and errors. AI-driven coding tools analyze clinical notes, extract relevant information, and assign appropriate billing codes with high accuracy. This streamlines the claim process, reduces denials, and increases revenue by ensuring that claims are submitted the first time correctly. By leveraging AI in billing and coding, practices can optimize their financial performance and reduce the administrative burden associated with these tasks.

AI is also enhancing patient communication. Advanced AI platforms can now handle a range of tasks, including answering patient inquiries via chatbots and scheduling appointments. These systems can provide immediate responses to patients, reducing wait times and improving patient satisfaction. Virtual assistants are also helping streamline patient intake and check-in processes by collecting demographic information and updating medical histories. These AI-driven systems free up staff to focus on more complex tasks, improving both patient care and operational efficiency.

The rise of wearable technology, such as smartwatches with ECG monitoring and continuous glucose monitoring devices, is another significant advancement. These devices are powered by AI algorithms that detect potential health issues and provide personalized insights to both patients and providers. These technologies allow for real-time tracking of patient health, which can inform clinical decision-making and improve patient outcomes. Wearables and remote patient monitoring provide a proactive approach to patient care, enabling providers to address health concerns before they escalate into more serious issues.

Robotic-assisted surgery is another area where technology is making a profound impact. Systems like the da Vinci Surgical System enable surgeons to perform minimally invasive procedures with enhanced precision and control, resulting in fewer complications and faster recovery times. In physical therapy, robotic exoskeletons are helping patients with mobility impairments regain movement and independence, further demonstrating the potential of robotics to improve patient outcomes.

The regulatory environment remains a persistent challenge for healthcare providers, with compliance requirements continually evolving. However, regulations can also present opportunities for those who take a proactive approach. Practices that invest in compliance training, risk management strategies, and streamlined documentation processes can reduce liability and improve overall efficiency. By staying informed and prepared, providers can leverage the regulatory landscape to their advantage and position themselves for long-term success.

Despite the complexities and challenges ahead, one fundamental truth remains: the core mission of healthcare, providing quality care to patients, will never change. The methods of delivering that care may evolve, but the commitment to improving lives will always be at the heart of the profession. Those who are willing to innovate, embrace new models, and adapt to the changing healthcare landscape will continue to find success, ensuring a sustainable future for their practices.

Key Takeaways:

- *The healthcare industry is rapidly evolving, with increasing consolidation, regulation, and financial pressures challenging traditional practice models.*

• *Adapting to value-based care, which focuses on patient outcomes and efficiency, will help practices thrive in the future healthcare landscape.*

• *Technology, including AI, telemedicine, remote monitoring, and digital health tools, is transforming healthcare practices and improving patient care.*

• *AI-driven medical scribing, billing, and patient communication tools can reduce administrative burdens, improve efficiency, and enhance patient satisfaction.*

• *Wearable technology and remote patient monitoring offer new ways to proactively manage patient health and make more informed clinical decisions.*

• *Staying informed and proactive in navigating the regulatory environment can help practices reduce liability and maintain operational efficiency.*

• *Despite the challenges, the core mission of providing quality care to patients remains central to the future success of healthcare providers.*

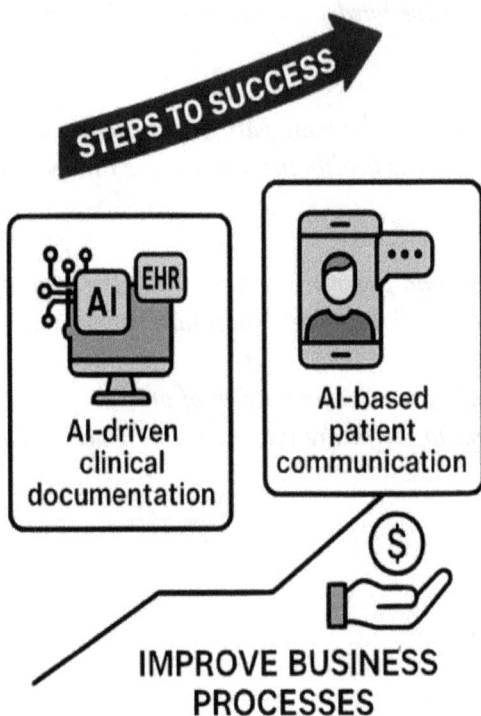

Tech Toys and Shiny New Things

STEPS TO SUCCESS

AI-driven clinical documentation

AI-based patient communication

IMPROVE BUSINESS PROCESSES

Chapter 16: Taking Care of Patients in a Virtual World

Since the COVID-19 pandemic, the rise of virtual clinical care has been steady and transformative. The convenience of interacting with healthcare providers on an as-needed basis has fueled the continued growth of telemedicine, offering a valuable tool for patient care. Patients appreciate the ability to consult with their doctors from the comfort of their homes, saving time and reducing the risk of exposure to illnesses. Providers, too, have embraced the flexibility it affords, allowing them to see more patients efficiently and reducing the burden of in-office visits. However, as with any healthcare innovation, sustainability depends on reimbursement models and the willingness of insurers and patients to recognize the value of these virtual encounters.

Initially, during the height of the pandemic, insurers expanded their telehealth coverage to encourage remote visits, offering reimbursement rates that closely mirrored those of in-person consultations. This temporary shift ensured continuity of care while minimizing the strain on hospitals and clinics. However, as the urgency of the pandemic receded, discussions about the long-term reimbursement structure for virtual visits intensified. The financial viability of telemedicine now hinges on whether payers continue to compensate providers at levels that reflect the time, expertise, and resources required for these visits.

If reimbursement remains close to that of an in-office visit, virtual care will continue to flourish. Patients will benefit from increased access to medical professionals, especially in rural areas where healthcare resources are scarce. Providers, in turn, will enjoy the ability to manage their schedules more effectively, reducing overhead costs associated with maintaining physical office space. Yet, the moment reimbursement rates drop to levels comparable to a phone consultation, the equation changes dramatically. At that point, the incentive for physicians to conduct virtual visits diminishes, as the financial return no longer justifies the effort. The convenience of telemedicine, however appealing, cannot come at the expense of undervaluing medical professionals' time and expertise.

The risk lies in allowing empathy and professional obligation to override financial sustainability. Physicians enter the field of medicine to help people, often prioritizing patient care over personal financial gain. However, a system that systematically undervalues telehealth services could lead to provider burnout and a decline in the quality of care. If payers recognize that doctors are willing to conduct virtual visits for minimal compensation, they may be tempted to continue reducing reimbursement rates, placing additional strain on practices. In turn, patients may begin to expect free or low-cost virtual access to their physicians, further eroding the financial foundation of telemedicine.

Real-world examples illustrate the precarious balance of virtual care adoption. Consider a primary care physician who, during the pandemic, transitioned a significant portion of their practice to telehealth. Initially, they found it to be a game-changer, as it allowed them to see more patients in less time, reduce no-show rates, and improve accessibility. However, when insurance companies later reduced payments for these visits, the physician faced a difficult choice: either see more patients for less money or revert to in-person visits, which came with higher operational costs but better reimbursement. Many providers find themselves in a similar situation, questioning the long-term feasibility of telemedicine if financial incentives dwindle.

For specialists, the issue becomes even more pronounced. A cardiologist conducting follow-up visits via telehealth may be able to offer the same level of care virtually as in-person, but if the reimbursement is significantly lower, the incentive to offer such visits disappears. Surgeons and orthopedic specialists face an even steeper challenge, as many aspects of their care require in-person evaluations, imaging studies, and hands-on assessments. If virtual follow-ups become less lucrative, specialists may feel compelled to limit their availability for such appointments, ultimately reducing patient options and delaying care.

The potential for virtual care is immense. As technology advances, remote monitoring, AI-assisted diagnostics, and digital therapeutics will likely enhance the effectiveness of telehealth. Wearable devices that track vital signs in real-time, integrated with telemedicine platforms, could enable even more comprehensive remote assessments. Patients managing chronic conditions, such as diabetes or hypertension, may benefit from real-time feedback, which reduces the need for frequent in-person visits while improving overall health outcomes. Yet, the promise of these advancements hinges on financial viability.

Some healthcare systems and private practices have begun exploring direct-to-consumer payment models, bypassing insurance reimbursement challenges. Concierge medicine, subscription-based tele-health services, and cash-pay virtual consultations offer alternatives for providers looking to maintain fair compensation for their services. While these models can work well for certain demographics, they may not be accessible to all patients, which could potentially exacerbate healthcare disparities. If telemedicine is to fulfill its promise of expanding access to care, it must remain financially viable within the insurance-based reimbursement framework that governs much of the U.S. healthcare system.

The challenge ahead is ensuring that virtual care remains an asset rather than a liability for providers. Policymakers, insurance companies, and healthcare professionals must collaborate to create sustainable reimbursement structures that recognize the value of telemedicine. If the industry fails to establish fair payment models, the rapid growth of virtual care could stall, and providers may retreat from offering these services. Ultimately, the goal should be to strike a balance, leveraging technology to improve patient outcomes while ensuring that medical professionals are adequately compensated for their expertise and time.

In the coming years, healthcare will likely continue evolving toward a hybrid model, blending in-person and virtual visits to optimize care delivery. Patients have grown accustomed to the convenience of tele-health, and many will continue to expect it as an option. However, the extent to which providers can embrace this shift will depend mainly on reimbursement policies. If payers recognize that tele-health is not just a temporary solution but a critical component of modern medicine, the industry will thrive. Conversely, if virtual visits become financially unsustainable for providers, the gains made in accessibility and efficiency may erode, leaving both patients and physicians frustrated with a system that failed to adapt.

Providers must remain vigilant in advocating for fair compensation, ensuring that the convenience of virtual care does not come at the cost of their professional worth. Otherwise, what began as a promising solution to modern healthcare challenges may become an underfunded, underutilized tool, one that benefits patients in theory but fails to support the very professionals who make it possible.

Key Takeaways:

• *Telemedicine Growth: Virtual care expanded rapidly during COVID-19 and continues to be valued for its convenience, accessibility, and efficiency.*

• *Reimbursement Challenges: The future of telehealth depends heavily on sustainable reimbursement rates. If payments drop too low, providers may be forced to reduce virtual services.*

• *Specialist Concerns: Specialists, particularly those needing in-person evaluations, face greater challenges in justifying virtual care if reimbursements decrease.*

• *Technology Opportunities: Advances like wearable devices and AI tools could enhance telehealth, but their success relies on maintaining financial viability.*

• *Alternative Payment Models: Some practices are exploring direct-to-consumer options, but these may not be equitable or widely accessible.*

• *Future Outlook: A hybrid model blending virtual and in-person care is likely, but its success depends on insurers recognizing telemedicine as essential and fairly compensating providers.*

• *Call to Action: Providers must advocate for fair reimbursement to ensure the long-term success and sustainability of virtual healthcare.*

Chapter 17: Providers at All Levels

The growth in both the scope of practice and utilization of Advanced Practice Providers (APPs) has expanded significantly over the years. As healthcare systems continue to evolve, incorporating APPs into your practice can be both cost-effective and beneficial for your patients. My daughter is a highly intelligent and successful physician associate (PA). When considering her options, including following my path through medical school, she worked and talked with PAs who worked for me. She found their profession and lifestyle aligned more with her career goals. She is an example of how capable and successful advanced practice providers can be.

However, caution must be taken to ensure their role is structured correctly within the practice. When used incorrectly, APPs can serve as a convenience but also an added expense, potentially leading to a loss of revenue rather than an increase. It is essential to have a well-thought-out strategy for their integration to maximize the impact on patient care and practice efficiency.

From a revenue generation perspective, advanced practice providers thrive in the clinical setting. Their ability to increase the number of patients a clinic can see in a day directly translates into financial benefits. By allowing for increased patient volume, they improve access to care, reduce appointment wait times, and enhance patient satisfaction. Patients often appreciate having more available options for scheduling, including same-day or walk-in appointments, which may not be feasible with a physician's schedule alone. This expanded access to care enhances the practice's overall functionality and productivity while keeping costs lower than hiring an additional physician.

For example, consider a busy orthopedic practice where patient volume exceeds the capacity of the available physicians. Without APPs, patients may have to wait weeks for an appointment, potentially leading them to seek care elsewhere. By incorporating advanced practice providers into the clinic, the practice can accommodate more patients, ensuring timely treatment, which in turn improves patient retention and satisfaction. A patient with a minor musculoskeletal injury can be assessed and treated by a APP without delay, while more complex cases can be referred to the physician. This efficient distribution of cases prevents unnecessary bottlenecks in scheduling and ensures that patients receive timely, appropriate care.

Advanced practice providers also play a significant role in increasing efficiency in hospital settings. In many hospitals, APPs make routine rounds on patients, assist with order placement, and help manage patient paperwork. This delegation of responsibilities allows physicians to focus on more complex cases, surgical procedures, or high-acuity patients who require specialized expertise. In a large healthcare system, for instance, a cardiologist may rely on APPs to handle routine inpatient follow-ups, medication adjustments, and discharge planning, thereby freeing up their time for new patient consultations or interventional procedures.

In surgical specialties, APPs can significantly enhance the efficiency of operating room schedules. In an orthopedic practice, for example, a physician associate (PA) or nurse practitioner (NP) can assist in surgery, helping with preoperative preparation, intraoperative tasks such as retraction or suturing, and postoperative care. This enables the surgeon to concentrate on the technical aspects of the procedure while ensuring a smooth workflow throughout the operation. Many surgical teams have found that integrating APPs into their workflow improves surgical efficiency, reduces turnover time between cases, and ultimately allows for a higher volume of surgeries to be performed within a given period.

Another crucial aspect of advanced practice provider utilization is their role in managing chronic disease and long-term patient care. Many primary care and specialty practices leverage APPs to conduct follow-up visits for patients with conditions such as diabetes, hypertension, or chronic pain. In a busy endocrinology practice, for example, APPs can oversee routine diabetes management, monitor lab results, adjust medications, and provide patient education, all of which improve outcomes while allowing physicians to focus on new diagnoses or complex cases. This model not only enhances patient care but also improves physician workflow and prevents burnout.

While the financial benefits of APPs are clear, there are also significant lifestyle and convenience advantages for physicians. In addition to their roles in the clinic and hospital, APPs can take on administrative responsibilities, including documentation, insurance pre-authorization, and coordinating care with other specialists. These tasks, while essential, can be time-consuming for physicians. By delegating tasks to advanced practice providers, physicians can allocate their time more effectively, improving their work-life balance and reducing the risk of burnout.

Consider the case of a solo practitioner managing a high-volume clinic. Without APP support, physicians are responsible for every aspect of patient care, from initial evaluation to follow-up visits, documentation, and administrative tasks. The workload can quickly become overwhelming, leading to extended hours, decreased job satisfaction, and increased stress. By integrating a APP into the practice, the physician can offload a portion of their patient encounters, delegate administrative responsibilities, and create a more sustainable work environment. This, in turn, leads to improved job satisfaction and longevity in practice.

There are also scenarios in which advanced practice providers can bridge gaps in care, particularly in rural or underserved areas. In many communities where physician shortages are a reality, APPs serve as the backbone of primary and specialty care. A rural family medicine clinic, for instance, may employ APPs to see the majority of routine patients while the physician focuses on complex cases or procedural work. This model enables the clinic to serve a larger patient population without overburdening a single physician, ensuring that essential healthcare services remain accessible in remote regions.

However, the successful integration of advanced practice providers requires a clear understanding of their role, appropriate supervision, and well-defined expectations. Practices must establish protocols for collaboration between physicians and APPs to ensure that patient care remains seamless and of high quality. There should also be a well-structured billing strategy to maximize reimbursement while maintaining compliance with regulatory guidelines. Improper utilization, such as having APPs see patients without appropriate oversight or billing incorrectly, can lead to decreased revenue or legal complications.

In one real-world example, a large multi-specialty practice struggled with declining revenue despite hiring multiple advanced practice providers. Upon closer analysis, it was found that APPs were primarily being utilized for tasks that did not significantly contribute to billable services. Rather than focusing on direct patient care, they were spending too much time on administrative duties, which, while helpful, did not justify their salaries in terms of revenue generation. After restructuring their roles to prioritize patient-facing encounters, particularly in acute illness or injury and chronic disease management, the practice saw a notable increase in revenue and overall efficiency.

To foster a strong and profitable relationship with APPs, practices should establish clear communication, transparency, and aligned incentives from the outset. This includes openly sharing relevant performance metrics, productivity benchmarks, and financial data so the provider understands how their work impacts the practice's bottom line. Implementing an incentive-based compensation model tied to measurable goals, such as patient volume, revenue generation, quality of care metrics, and patient satisfaction, can align their interests with those of the practice. Regular reviews of both clinical and financial performance help identify opportunities for improvement, reinforce accountability, and ensure that the provider remains both clinically valuable and financially beneficial to the organization.

Ultimately, determining how to best utilize advanced practice providers is an individual practice decision. There is no one-size-fits-all model, and successful integration depends on the specific needs and goals of the practice. Whether the primary objective is financial growth, improved efficiency, expanded access to care, or better work-life balance for physicians, APPs can play a crucial role in achieving those goals when implemented correctly. The key lies in understanding what the practice aims to accomplish and structuring the APPs' responsibilities accordingly.

As the healthcare landscape continues to evolve, APPs will remain a valuable asset in many settings. Their ability to improve patient access, enhance workflow efficiency, and support physician productivity makes them an essential component of modern medical practice. However, thoughtful planning, strategic deployment, and ongoing evaluation are crucial to ensuring that their presence positively impacts both patient outcomes and the overall success of the practice.

Key Takeaways

• *Advanced Practice Providers (APPs) (PAs and NPs) can greatly enhance practice efficiency, patient access, and revenue when properly integrated.*

• *Strategic role structuring is critical; misuse can lead to increased costs and lost revenue.*

• *APPs expand patient capacity by handling routine care, urgent visits, and chronic disease management, freeing physicians for complex cases.*

• *In surgical and hospital settings, APPs enhance workflow, mitigate physician burnout, and facilitate improved surgical scheduling and patient care coordination.*

• *Clear supervision, billing strategies, and defined responsibilities are essential to maximize both financial and patient care benefits.*

• *Successful integration depends on the specific goals of the practice; there is no one-size-fits-all approach.*

Part Three:
Parts, People, and Principles

Chapter 18: End of the Status Quo

There is no doubt that medicine is changing. New ways to practice continue to emerge. Reimbursement models are changing, and traditional payment methods are slowly disappearing. Insurance payers are altering the metrics used to determine reimbursement and payments. This creates an ever-changing and uncertain environment in the current practice of medicine. In addition, new laws and regulations continue to impose burdens of time, paperwork, and compliance on providers and their practices. Add the increasing cost of employees and general business expenses, and you can see how challenging the current climate can be. However, even in an unstable environment, you can find areas of excellent opportunity. You just have to be willing to look and think creatively.

Many take the road of negativity. Discouraged by the change, they complain about the challenges and look back on past days with longing. But in reality, that does nothing to help where you are. To achieve success, you must seek out new opportunities and then pursue them. Some efforts will falter, others will flourish, and the secret is simple: persistence is the path, success the destination.

There is something to be said for resilience and adaptability in times of rapid transformation. Those who resist change often find themselves in a perpetual cycle of frustration, stuck in the past while the world moves forward. The landscape of medicine has never been static, and those who understand this reality have come to embrace the field's evolution rather than resist it. Change has always been a fundamental part of medical practice, from the advent of new technologies to shifts in healthcare policy. The key is to approach it not as a challenge to be feared but as an opportunity to be seized.

Consider the shifting nature of reimbursement. In the past, traditional fee-for-service models were the norm. Physicians were compensated based on the number of patients seen, tests ordered, or procedures performed. However, the landscape is shifting toward value-based care, where reimbursement is tied to outcomes and efficiency rather than volume. Many practitioners view this as an obstacle, a complex system that creates more hurdles to navigate. But within this change lies an opportunity to redefine practice efficiency and patient engagement. Those who adapt by focusing on preventative care, patient education, and streamlined operations will find themselves ahead of the curve rather than scrambling to keep up.

The regulatory burden is another concern that looms large over the industry. Compliance with new laws, maintaining extensive documentation, and ensuring that practices align with ever-evolving guidelines can be exhausting. Many providers find themselves buried under administrative tasks, leaving less time for patient care. But instead of seeing this as an insurmountable roadblock, those with a forward-thinking mindset recognize the potential advantages. By leveraging technology, such as electronic health records and artificial intelligence-driven administrative tools, practices can mitigate the workload and improve efficiency. Telemedicine, for example, was once viewed as a niche service, but it has now evolved into a powerful tool that enables physicians to expand their reach, reduce overhead, and enhance patient satisfaction.

The rising costs associated with running a medical practice are yet another factor contributing to the changing climate. The expenses tied to staffing, equipment, rent, and insurance continue to increase. While this presents a legitimate challenge, it also forces innovation. Many providers are turning to collaborative practice models, merging with other practices or joining management services organizations to distribute costs and increase negotiating power. This shift creates a more sustainable business model where financial strain is lessened, allowing physicians to focus on delivering quality care rather than struggling to keep their doors open.

Embracing a business mindset is becoming more critical in modern medicine. Physicians, traditionally trained to focus solely on patient care, now find themselves in positions where understanding the economics of healthcare is essential. Financial literacy, operational efficiency, and strategic growth planning are no longer optional; they are critical skills. Those who take the time to educate themselves on these aspects will be better positioned to navigate the evolving landscape.

Beyond the financial aspects, there is also an opportunity in redefining the patient experience. The modern patient is more informed and engaged than ever before. They seek out providers who offer not only medical expertise but also accessibility, convenience, and a personalized approach. Practices that adopt this shift by implementing patient portals, mobile communication tools, and holistic care models will foster stronger relationships with their patients, resulting in increased loyalty and improved health outcomes. The traditional doctor-patient relationship is evolving, and those who understand the importance of patient engagement will thrive in this new era.

It is also important to recognize the role of innovation in medical practice. The integration of artificial intelligence, precision medicine, and wearable health technology is revolutionizing healthcare delivery. Rather than fearing these advancements, providers should explore how these tools can enhance diagnostics, treatment planning, and patient monitoring. Those who stay informed and integrate these innovations into their practice will not only remain competitive but also improve patient care in ways previously unimaginable.

Of course, change is never without risk. There will be setbacks, and not every new approach will lead to immediate success. But that is the nature of progress. The ability to assess, adapt, and refine strategies is what separates those who flourish from those who falter. Fear of failure often prevents people from taking the necessary steps toward growth. Yet, every major advancement in medicine, from surgical techniques to pharmaceutical breakthroughs, was born from trial and error. The same principle applies to navigating the modern healthcare environment.

Ultimately, the secret to success in today's medical field is a mindset shift. Instead of viewing change as a threat, it must be seen as an invitation to innovate. Those who embrace the new possibilities, who are willing to take calculated risks, and who remain adaptable in their approach will be the ones who succeed. The landscape of medicine will continue to evolve, just as it always has. The question is not whether change will come, but rather how one chooses to respond to it. Those who take an active role in shaping their future, rather than passively reacting to external forces, will find themselves in a position of strength and stability.

As with any major shift, there will always be voices of doubt, those who lament the "good old days" and resist moving forward. However, history has shown time and time again that those who remain stagnant are ultimately left behind. In contrast, those who are willing to explore new paths, embrace innovation, and push beyond their comfort zones will continue to find opportunities where others see only obstacles. Medicine is not a static field; it is a living, evolving entity that demands adaptability. The most successful practitioners are not necessarily those with the most years of experience, but those who are willing to continue learning, growing, and evolving along with the field.

There is no perfect roadmap to navigating the future of healthcare. Each practice, each provider, will have its own journey, shaped by unique circumstances and challenges. But the common thread among those who thrive will always be a proactive mindset. Instead of lamenting the complexities of modern medicine, they will explore new business models, leverage technology, and prioritize patient-centered care. They will seek out collaborations, continuously educate themselves, and remain open to change.

The future of medicine belongs to those who are willing to embrace it. While the road ahead may be uncertain, it is also full of possibilities. Success will not come to those who wait for things to return to how they once were, it will come to those who forge ahead, unafraid to innovate and take bold steps toward the future. The choice is clear: remain stuck in the past or step forward and take control of the opportunities that change brings. The practitioners who make that choice with confidence and determination will be the ones who define the future of medicine. To become successful, you must look for new openings and then pursue them. Remember, some efforts will falter, others will flourish, and the secret is simple: persistence is the path, success the destination.

Key Takeaways:

- *Medicine Is Rapidly Evolving: Changes in reimbursement models, regulations, and business costs are reshaping the medical landscape.*

- *Adaptability Is Critical: Providers who embrace change and innovate will thrive, while those who resist will struggle to succeed.*

- *Shift to Value-Based Care: Success depends on focusing on outcomes, efficiency, preventative care, and patient engagement rather than volume.*

- *Technology Is an Asset: Leveraging tools such as telemedicine, AI, and electronic health records can ease administrative burdens and enhance care.*
- *Collaboration Strengthens Practices: Joining management service organizations (MSOs) or adopting collaborative models can help alleviate financial pressures.*

- *Business Skills Are Essential: Financial literacy, operational efficiency, and strategic growth are now necessary skills for physicians.*

- *Patient-Centered Care Is Key: Modern patients expect accessibility, convenience, and a personalized experience.*

- *Innovation Drives Success: Embracing advancements such as wearable technology, AI, and precision medicine will keep practices competitive and ahead of the curve.*

- *Mindset Matters Most: Viewing change as an opportunity, not a threat, and staying resilient through failures leads to long-term success.*

Chapter 19: A Matter of Principle

Success in medicine is not guaranteed, but certain principles can stack the deck in your favor. By following these core guidelines, you can build a strong foundation for both professional and financial success. These are not just rules; they are the framework for a career that is both fulfilling and sustainable. If you are looking for the secret to long-term success in medicine, start here.

Principle #1: Take Care of Your Patients

This principle may seem obvious, yet it is often overlooked. In the pursuit of success, whether financial or professional, some providers cut corners when it comes to patient care. While this may yield short-term gains, it will ultimately lead to failure.

Patients talk. Providers talk. Insurance carriers talk. Attorneys talk. Word spreads quickly, and if you develop a reputation for subpar care, it will come back to haunt you. Your goal should be to provide the best care possible, not just because it is the ethical and correct thing to do, but also because it is the best long-term business strategy. Patients who trust you will return to you. They will refer their friends and family to you. They will become your best advocates, marketing you better than any ad campaign ever could.

The most successful medical practices are built on trust and quality care. If you take the time to listen to your patients genuinely, address their concerns, and consistently provide top-tier care, you will develop a reputation that will serve you well. Many providers make the mistake of focusing too much on operational efficiency at the expense of the patient experience. While efficiency is important, it should never come at the cost of care. Patients notice when they are being rushed, ignored, or treated as a number instead of a person.

A strong reputation for quality care does not just attract patients; it also attracts the right kind of staff. Talented professionals want to work for organizations that prioritize excellence and ethics. If your practice is recognized for prioritizing patient care, you will find it easier to attract and retain high-quality team members who share your values.

Additionally, consider how technological advancements and patient communication strategies can improve the care experience. Telemedicine, electronic medical records, and automated appointment reminders can enhance patient engagement, but they should never replace the human touch. A warm, attentive bedside manner and a genuine interest in patients' well-being go further than any technology ever could.

The key takeaway: If patient care is not the most important factor in your decision-making, your success will be short-lived. Take care of your patients, and they will take care of you.

Principle #2: Value Your Time

Time is your most precious asset. It is the only resource that you can never get back. Too often, healthcare providers undervalue their own time, giving it away for free or allowing others to dictate how it is used. You do not have to give away your time to prove you are a good provider or a good person. Many well-intentioned providers spend hours on unnecessary tasks, such as free consultations or administrative burdens, that could be outsourced or better managed. This is not only a personal drain but also a business mistake. Your time has value, and if you do not protect it, others will take advantage of it.

Consider how you spend your workday. Are you focusing on high-value activities, or are you bogged down with tasks that do not contribute to your growth or success? Learn to delegate, automate, or eliminate low-value tasks. Use your time to improve patient care, enhance your practice, or develop new revenue streams.

Most importantly, do not allow yourself to be taken advantage of. Set boundaries. Respect your schedule. Charge appropriately for your expertise and services. If you do not value your time, no one else will.

Beyond just protecting your schedule, you should also optimize it. If you are spending an excessive amount of time on redundant paperwork, consider investing in more efficient Electronic Medical Record (EMR) systems that can streamline your workflow. If billing and insurance claims are eating into your clinical hours, consider hiring a billing specialist. Every minute spent on administrative tasks is a minute not spent on patient care or business growth.

Furthermore, providers should not be afraid to say no. If a task does not align with your priorities, delegate it or eliminate it. Overcommitting can lead to burnout, ultimately impacting your ability to provide quality care.

The key takeaway: Treat your time as your most valuable asset. Protect it, use it wisely, and ensure it is being spent on activities that will bring you long-term success.

Principle #3: Improve or Take Advantage of What You Already Do or Provide.

Innovation is not just about creating something brand new. Many people get caught up in the idea that success comes from discovering the next big thing. While new innovations can be valuable, success often stems from improving or leveraging existing processes.

Look at your current practice. What treatments, services, or recommendations do you already provide? What products do you frequently prescribe or use? Instead of looking for something completely novel, find ways to optimize and expand what is already working for you.

For example, if you regularly recommend a particular type of medical equipment, consider working with a supplier to provide that equipment directly to your patients. If you specialize in a particular procedure, look for ways to refine or enhance it to provide better outcomes and differentiate yourself from competitors.

Owning or controlling aspects of your existing practice can create new revenue streams and reduce dependence on external companies. This is not about compromising patient care; it's about ensuring that the things you already do work better for both you and your patients.

Additionally, consider how strategic partnerships can enhance your existing services. Collaborating with specialists, physical therapists, or other healthcare providers can create a more comprehensive care experience for your patients while also benefiting your practice financially.

The key takeaway: You do not have to reinvent the wheel. Start by optimizing what you already do. Improve your current services, take control of key elements of your practice, and build success from what you already know.

Principle #4: Don't Be Afraid to Fail

Fear of failure holds more people back than anything else. If you never try, you will never succeed. Every successful person has a long history of failures behind them. The difference is that they kept going.

Failure is not the end; it is a lesson. Many of the most successful individuals in medicine and business have stories of ventures that did not work out. Some failed at great financial or personal cost. However, each failure provided valuable knowledge, experience, and resilience that ultimately led to greater success in the long run.

If you prefer to stay within your comfort zone, work your regular shift hours, and earn a steady paycheck, that's perfectly fine. There is nothing wrong with that path. Just do not complain about financial limitations or lack of opportunity if you are unwilling to take risks. Success requires effort, resilience, and the ability to persevere in the face of setbacks. If you want to be extraordinary, you have to do extraordinary things.

If you want to create something bigger for yourself, whether it is a thriving medical practice, financial freedom, or a new business venture, you have to be willing to fail. Every attempt teaches you something new, and every setback prepares you for the next opportunity.

Consider risk as an investment. Calculated risks are necessary for growth. This does not mean reckless decision-making, but rather making informed choices with a willingness to learn from the outcomes. Failure in one area often opens doors in another.

The key takeaway: Fear of failure will hold you back more than failure itself. Take calculated risks, learn from mistakes, and keep pushing forward. Success is not guaranteed, but it is achievable for those who are willing to put in the work.

The FOUR PRINCIPLES of SUCCESS in MEDICINE

PRINCIPLE #1
Take Care of your Patients
Provide top-tier care and build trust with patients.

PRINCIPLE #2
Value Your Time
Treat time as a valuable asset and focus on high-value activities

PRINCIPLE #3
Improve or Take Advantage of What You Already Do or Provide
Enhance and leverage existing services and treatments.

PRINCIPLE #4
Do Not Be Afraid to Fail
Take risks, learn from mistakes and keep pushing forward.

Chapter 20: Stuck in the System

While this book has focused primarily on providers in private practice, many of the core principles and techniques discussed can also be applied to the employed practice model. Employed providers often feel restricted, as they are unable to make significant changes or decisions due to the nature of their contracts and the organizational structure. And while it's true that you may not be the one calling the shots, that doesn't mean you're powerless. You may not control policies or budgets, but you can still influence outcomes and find ways to succeed.

Begin by exploring the administrative or leadership roles that may exist within your organization. Larger systems often have committees, department meetings, or strategic groups that require input from physicians. Volunteering for a medical director role, participating in a quality improvement team, or helping with workflow redesign can give you a seat at the table, one that allows you to shape decision-making and drive improvements. Even more minor roles, such as becoming the point person for a new electronic health record feature rollout or coordinating continuing medical education for your team, can establish you as a leader and create opportunities.

Rather than approaching administration as the enemy, position yourself as an ally. The traditional tension between providers and administrators, cost versus care, productivity versus workflow, doesn't have to be your reality. Utilize your clinical expertise to help the administration achieve goals that matter to both parties. For example, if you notice bottlenecks in scheduling or patient flow, propose a new triage or check-in process to address these issues. Suggest evidence-based changes that can increase throughput without compromising care. Administrators are often more receptive than we assume, especially when ideas are presented with data or framed in terms of increased revenue, patient satisfaction, or decreased cost.

Let's say you're a hospital-employed orthopedic surgeon and you notice your OR block times are inefficient, leading to delays and lower volume. Instead of simply complaining, gather data, talk to the schedulers and staff, and present a solution. Recommend changes that streamline prep and turnover time. Offer to pilot the new process. Now you're not just identifying problems, you're driving value.

Bring the same mindset to billing and coding. Many employed providers are unaware of how they're being billed or who is performing the coding. This is a mistake. Take time to review how your services are being coded and submitted. Request a chart audit or ask to sit down with someone from the billing department. In some cases, you may find missed charges, under-coding, or delays that are costing both you and the organization revenue. By addressing these issues, you're increasing efficiency and income, two key objectives that leadership always strives for.

Explore whether your organization has any profit-sharing or performance-based incentive programs. Many systems have funds earmarked for innovation, efficiency projects, or improvements in patient satisfaction. If your idea can show a return on investment, financial or in terms of improved outcomes, you might be surprised how quickly you can gain support. For example, if you're in a multispecialty clinic and have an idea to incorporate AI-based documentation tools that reduce charting time, put together a proposal that shows the cost of implementation, estimated time savings, and the impact on physician burnout. If the organization sees a clear benefit, there's a good chance they'll consider it.

Side business ventures can sometimes still be pursued within an employment model, depending on the terms of your contract. Some contracts permit outside consulting, teaching, research, or even ownership in ancillary services, such as imaging or physical therapy. Review your agreement or consult a healthcare attorney to determine what is permitted. If there's room to create a speaking business, offer CME courses, or participate in innovation projects, go for it. Your expertise has real value beyond your daily clinical duties.

Also, take the time to advocate for the implementation of new technologies discussed earlier in this book. Whether it's adopting digital check-in systems, remote monitoring tools, or virtual rehab platforms, your leadership in introducing these tools shows initiative. Organizations may initially hesitate due to cost, but if you can demonstrate how a specific tool leads to better patient outcomes or reduced staff burden, you can build a strong case for adoption. Many institutions are hungry for solutions; they need someone to connect the dots.

Ultimately, if you find yourself consistently at odds with your employer, ignored in meetings, and dissatisfied despite your efforts, it may be time to ask a difficult question: Is this the right place for me? The choice between private practice and employed practice is deeply personal. It depends on your values, tolerance for risk, lifestyle, and long-term goals. Some providers thrive within structured systems, enjoying the stability and resources they offer. Others feel stifled and crave the autonomy of running their own show.

Neither path is inherently right or wrong; it's about what works best for you. But even in an employed model, you have more power than you think. You can influence, lead, innovate, and build a career that is both fulfilling and impactful. Don't assume you're stuck just because you're part of the system. There are plenty of ways to rise within it, or to leverage your position into the next great opportunity.

Chapter 21: It's All About the Team

One of the most important lessons I've learned in my professional journey is that success is rarely achieved in isolation. The best way to achieve real, sustainable success is to surround yourself with great people. This may sound like common sense, but in practice, especially in healthcare, it's a lesson that's often overlooked.

Surrounding yourself with great people means building a team of experts who excel in specific areas. It means intentionally filling the gaps in your knowledge and skillset with individuals whose strengths complement your own. When done right, this approach not only elevates your performance but also elevates everyone involved.

Adopting a team-based success mindset can be surprisingly challenging in the healthcare world. Many healthcare providers are high achievers. They've spent years, sometimes decades, in rigorous education and training. They've been top of their class in medical school, completed challenging residencies or fellowships, and are often recognized as leaders in their specialties. They're used to being the most educated, most knowledgeable person in the room. And that's no small accomplishment.

But therein lies the challenge. Due to the nature of medical education and clinical leadership, many providers have become accustomed to being the authority. In clinical settings, this makes perfect sense; the physician must lead with confidence and knowledge. However, this same mindset can create blind spots when it comes to managing the non-clinical side of a practice. In many cases, this well-earned confidence can inadvertently evolve into aloofness or even arrogance, particularly when it comes to the business aspects of running a practice. It's not necessarily intentional, but it can hinder growth. It can make it harder to admit when help is needed or to accept that someone else might know more in a specific non-clinical area.

This is a critical mistake. The truth is that no one can excel at everything. Even the most brilliant surgeon or diagnostician may not fully grasp the nuances of billing codes, payer contracts, or revenue cycle management. And that's okay. What matters is having the humility to recognize those gaps, and the wisdom to fill them with the right people.

I speak from experience when I say that humbling yourself, admitting what you don't know, and building a team that may be more experienced or knowledgeable in key operational areas is one of the smartest decisions you can make. It's a shift in mindset, from trying to carry the whole load yourself to strategically delegating and trusting experts to help you build something stronger, more sustainable, and more successful.

Let's take finance as a concrete example. I understand a profit and loss statement. I can read a balance sheet. I know the basics of how my business is doing. But that's only scratching the surface. To truly understand what's driving my expenses up or what's suppressing revenue, I need expert insight. That's where my financial team comes in. They don't just give me raw numbers, they provide context, insight, and actionable data. They help me see what's going on beneath the surface so I can make smart, informed decisions.

This same concept applies to every major area of practice management, including contracting, compliance, marketing, human resources, billing, and IT; the list goes on. You may know enough to ask questions or to recognize when something seems off. But if you don't have someone who lives and breathes that subject matter, you're putting yourself and your practice at a disadvantage.

This is especially critical in today's healthcare landscape. With increasing administrative complexity, evolving reimbursement models, and rising patient expectations, running a successful healthcare practice is more challenging than ever. It's not enough to just be a great clinician; you have to be a competent business owner, too. And unless you have a background in healthcare management, you'll almost certainly need help with that.

Yet I'm continually surprised by how many providers are trying to do it all themselves.

Far too often, I step into a practice that's struggling, not because the provider isn't skilled or committed, but because they're trying to wear too many hats. They're making clinical decisions, managing staff, negotiating contracts, overseeing billing, handling marketing, and usually doing all of this with the help of one office manager or assistant, if that. It's an exhausting, unsustainable way to run a business. And it almost always leads to burnout, missed opportunities, or both.

I want to be clear: I understand that not every practice can afford a large, complex management team. However, every practice, regardless of its size, must have a qualified and appropriately scaled management structure. It's about investing wisely, not extravagantly. A small practice might not need a full-time CFO, but it may benefit from a financial consultant or an outsourced billing specialist. A solo provider might not need a marketing department. Still, they could see significant returns from working with a part-time strategist or a reputable firm that specializes in healthcare marketing.

The goal isn't to build a massive team. It's to build the right team. A team that fits the size, scope, and goals of your practice, and that brings expertise in areas where you need support.

Let me tell you why this matters so much: when you have experts around you, you make better decisions. You act with more clarity and confidence. You avoid costly mistakes. You identify opportunities you might have missed. And perhaps most importantly, you give yourself the freedom to focus on what you do best, taking care of patients.

Think about it. Every hour you spend chasing down unpaid claims or negotiating lease renewals is an hour not spent with patients. Every minute you spend updating your website or trying to interpret labor laws is a minute you're not focused on clinical excellence. And those trade-offs add up. Over time, they drain your energy, limit your growth, and undermine the quality of care you can provide.

Delegation isn't about laziness; it's about leverage. It's about putting the right people in the right roles so you can maximize your impact and lead more effectively. It's about recognizing that great leaders aren't the ones who try to do everything; they're the ones who build great teams.

It also creates a culture of mutual respect. When you surround yourself with capable professionals and treat them as trusted partners, you send a clear message: I value your expertise and appreciate your contributions. I trust your judgment. I need your insight. That kind of respect is powerful. It motivates people. It fosters loyalty. It encourages collaboration. And it sets the tone for a healthy, high-performing organization.

Let's not forget the emotional and mental health aspect of all this. Running a medical practice is incredibly demanding. The pressure, the stakes, the constant juggling, it takes a toll. Having a strong team isn't just about better business outcomes. It's about building a support system. It's about creating a work environment where you're not alone in the struggle, where you can share the load, and where you can lean on others when things get tough.

This is particularly relevant in the current era, where burnout and stress levels among healthcare professionals have reached alarming highs. We need to rethink how we structure our practices. We need to stop glorifying the "do-it-all" provider and start celebrating the collaborative leader. We need to recognize that strength isn't about knowing everything; it's about knowing when to ask for help.

So, how do you start building this kind of team? First, take stock of your current operation. Where are the gaps? What tasks are falling through the cracks or being done inefficiently? What decisions are you making without enough information or support? Be honest with yourself. Then, start small. Identify one or two areas where targeted assistance could make a significant impact. Maybe it's hiring a billing specialist. Perhaps it's bringing in a part-time HR consultant. Maybe it's outsourcing your marketing. Whatever it is, take that first step.

Then, keep building. Stay open. Stay humble. Don't be afraid to say, "I don't know." Say, "I need help." Say, "I trust you." And watch how your practice transforms.

The bottom line is this: success in healthcare today requires more than clinical expertise. It requires business savvy, operational excellence, and strategic thinking. No one person can do all of these things alone. Surround yourself with great people. People who are smarter than you in specific areas. People who challenge you, support you, and help you grow. Build a team that raises the bar, and let them help you raise your own.

Chapter 22: A Word on Leadership

It is time to give some attention to how you lead. To achieve success, everything we have discussed so far is important. However, how you lead your team and implement these strategies is just as vital, if not even more critical. Leadership is the invisible engine behind every action, every goal, and every outcome. It shapes the culture, the pace, the standards, and ultimately the results. If leadership falters, even the best ideas, plans, and resources can be wasted.

I have always been a supporter of a leadership style that emphasizes respect, compassion, and getting hands-on to do the work alongside the team. Leading by example, in my mind, is one of the most powerful methods to earn genuine respect. Kindness can inspire people. When respect is earned through authenticity, not demanded by authority, the environment changes. People feel safer, more creative, and more motivated to put themselves out there for you. They are willing to take risks, to think differently, and to give more of themselves because they feel supported rather than judged.

I do believe that this style can work and can yield tremendous benefits. Some of the most rewarding experiences I have had in my career stemmed from teams that operated under this style of leadership. I have seen people who may have been overlooked or underestimated elsewhere blossom into high-performing, creative, and integral team members simply because they were given a little trust and support. This environment allows people to feel like they have ownership, like their ideas matter, and that they are valued not just for their output but for who they are as individuals.

However, it would be naive not to acknowledge that there are real downsides to this approach as well. People tend to default to the path of least resistance and the easiest effort. It's human nature to conserve energy unless something pushes us otherwise. When leadership relies too heavily on kindness and support without sufficient structure or expectations, some individuals will inevitably start to push those boundaries. They may take advantage of the leniency. Deadlines begin to slip. Accountability softens.

Quality can start to diminish. What's worse is that high-performing team members may start to feel frustrated if they see that underperformance is tolerated. Eventually, the very culture that was meant to lift everyone starts to erode from within. It doesn't happen overnight, but slowly, silently, it creeps in if left unchecked.

With a less demanding style, the leader can fall into the trap of becoming more of a peer or a buddy than a boss. While friendships and strong relationships are valuable, the danger lies in blurred lines of authority. When challenging moments arise, because they always do, it becomes much harder to have the tough conversations that are necessary for the team's health and the mission's success. Without clear standards and consequences, even well-intentioned teams can drift into mediocrity.

The counter to this style is the more stereotypical corporate boss leadership style, the "I'm not your friend" approach. This leader is highly demanding, focused primarily on performance, results, and accountability. Relationships take a back seat to efficiency. In this style, the leader drives the team with clear expectations, tight deadlines, and little room for error. Mistakes are not learning opportunities but failures to be corrected swiftly. Often, this creates a high-pressure environment that runs hot and hard, pushing people to their limits.

In my experience, although this style can create stress and dissatisfaction among employees, it can also be undeniably successful from a purely performance-based standpoint. High expectations yield high output. Processes become streamlined. There's little tolerance for waste, for inefficiency, or subpar work. People may fear the leader, but that fear drives a particular kind of focus. Under this style, I have seen teams produce incredible work, hitting targets that would have been otherwise out of reach under a softer leadership approach.

But success in output does not always mean long-term health for the organization. Over time, high stress and fear-based environments cause cracks to form. Employee turnover spikes. Creativity dries up because people become afraid to take risks. Innovation stalls because no one wants to stick their neck out and be punished for a misstep. Customer experience can suffer because unhappy employees often project that dissatisfaction outward. Eventually, the organization becomes a machine, high-functioning, yes, but brittle and prone to collapse when faced with challenges that require adaptability, creativity, or sustained human engagement.

I have experienced all these issues myself. I have experienced the consequences of both leadership styles, including both the highs and the lows. Through this, I have had to develop a hybrid style of leadership, a blend that maintains the values of compassion and respect, while also incorporating the rigor of high standards and accountability. In this hybrid model, I still believe in leading by example. I still get into the trenches with my team. I still foster an environment where creativity is encouraged, and mistakes are seen as opportunities for learning.

However, I am much more direct now. I do not shy away from uncomfortable conversations. When performance slips, it is addressed immediately, clearly, and respectfully. Expectations are stated openly and revisited regularly. Assignments come with deadlines that are not suggestions but commitments. Accountability is no longer optional; it is built into the very fabric of how we operate. And when necessary, disciplinary measures are taken, not punitively, but as part of maintaining the integrity of the team and the mission.

This hybrid approach allows me to hold people to a high standard without creating an atmosphere of fear. People know they are valued, but they also know that their performance matters, not just their intentions. They understand that mistakes are tolerated, but laziness and carelessness are not. They see that kindness does not mean a lack of expectations, and that respect goes both ways: I respect their individuality and effort, and they, in turn, respect the structure and the mission.

One example that stands out to me was a project we undertook that required significant innovation. If I had led purely with the demanding, corporate boss style, I am confident the project would have been completed on time and under budget, but it would have lacked the creative spark that ultimately made it a success. People would have been too afraid to take the risks needed to innovate. On the other hand, if I had led purely with the softer, supportive style, we might have generated a lot of great ideas, but we would have lacked execution and missed deadlines. It was only by blending the two approaches, encouraging creativity but anchoring it with clear deadlines and non-negotiable deliverables, that we achieved something truly remarkable.

There was another occasion when I saw firsthand how a hybrid model saved a struggling department. Morale was low, and turnover was high. The previous leadership had been extremely harsh, driving people relentlessly without any regard for their well-being. Initially, I focused heavily on rebuilding trust, listening attentively, showing compassion, and giving people space to feel valued again. It helped, but it wasn't enough. Performance was still lagging. I had to pivot and introduce clear metrics, regular performance reviews, and real accountability measures. It wasn't always comfortable, but within six months, the department had turned around, not just in terms of output, but also in employee satisfaction.

I have also discovered that different individuals respond uniquely to various leadership styles. Some people excel under pressure and tight deadlines; others perform their best when they feel fully supported and encouraged. The hybrid model offers flexibility. I can adjust my approach slightly depending on the needs of the individual and the demands of the moment, all while maintaining focus on the overarching principles.

The reality is, no single leadership style is perfect. Pure compassion without accountability can lead to mediocrity. Pure discipline without humanity can lead to burnout and resentment. Success lies somewhere in the balance, leading with kindness but not weakness, holding high standards without becoming heartless, and allowing room for creativity while maintaining focus and direction.

Leadership is, at its core, a relationship. Like all relationships, it requires trust, communication, and mutual respect. It requires an understanding that people are not robots; they are emotional, complex, and driven by more than just fear or ambition. They need to feel that what they do matters, that their leader sees them, values them, and believes in their potential, while also holding them responsible for living up to that potential.

It is a balancing act that requires constant attention, adjustment, and humility. I have made mistakes, learned from them, and continue to refine my approach. Leadership is not a static thing you master once and then forget about. It is dynamic, evolving with each new team, each new challenge, and each new opportunity.

Ultimately, the goal is not just to lead a team to success on a single project or a single quarter's performance. It is to build an environment where success is sustainable, where people continually grow, and where work has meaning beyond just numbers on a page. It is about creating something lasting, something worth being part of, and something that can weather the inevitable storms that come with any worthwhile endeavor.

Leadership is hard. It is messy. It demands more from you than it does from anyone else, but when done right, it is also one of the most rewarding experiences imaginable. Leadership starts with the willingness to lead not just from the front, but from the heart, with both strength and compassion, with both vision and discipline, and with a commitment to never stop learning how to do it better.

Chapter 23: Final Thoughts
There Are No Secrets

The secret to success in medicine is not a single formula or a lucky break. It is built on a foundation of strong principles. Taking care of your patients, valuing your time, improving what you already do, and embracing failure as part of the journey are all essential components. These principles will not only make you a better healthcare provider but also open doors to greater financial and professional success. But success is not solely measured by financial gains or career achievements. True success in medicine and life is multifaceted, encompassing personal fulfillment, meaningful relationships, and a sense of purpose.

Success in medicine, just like in any other field, is not easy. It takes work, strategy, and persistence. But it is possible. If you apply these principles consistently, you will not only survive in this industry, but you will thrive. However, it is essential to recognize that thriving is not solely about the number of patients you see, the revenue you generate, or the prestige you achieve. It is about finding balance, meaning, and joy in what you do every day. Many people enter the field of medicine believing that financial success and professional accolades are the ultimate measures of achievement. While these can be indicators of hard work and dedication, they do not define the entirety of success.

Happiness is a crucial component of success, and it is not solely derived from wealth or status. Many highly accomplished physicians find themselves burned out, disillusioned, and disconnected from what once inspired them. This is because they have placed too much emphasis on external achievements and not enough on internal fulfillment. True happiness comes from finding purpose in your work, maintaining meaningful relationships, and achieving a sense of balance between your professional and personal life. Success should not come at the expense of health, family, or personal peace. No amount of professional recognition or financial reward can compensate for a life lived without fulfillment and purpose.

Lifestyle plays a significant role in defining success. A physician who is constantly overworked, exhausted, and unable to spend time with family and friends may be financially successful, but emotionally and spiritually depleted.

The ability to enjoy time with loved ones, engage in hobbies, and maintain good physical and mental health is as important as professional achievement. A balanced life leads to greater overall well-being, allowing one to bring more energy, compassion, and excellence into their medical practice. It is essential to set boundaries and prioritize what truly matters, as this will lead to a more sustainable and fulfilling career.

One of the most rewarding aspects of practicing medicine is the opportunity to serve a higher calling. The ability to heal, comfort, and guide patients through some of their most challenging moments is a privilege that goes beyond any material gain. Treating patients with respect, compassion, and a genuine commitment to their well-being is what builds true success.

Patients remember the care they receive, the kindness they are shown, and the trust they build with their physicians. Reputation is not just about professional achievements but about the impact left on the lives of those served. Every patient encounter is an opportunity to make a difference, and it is here that the most profound fulfillment in medicine is found.

For me, my relationship with Christ drives my business decisions and directs my care of patients. My faith provides a foundation for my work, guiding my interactions and reinforcing the importance of integrity, humility, and service. Success is not just about personal gain but about living out a purpose that aligns with my beliefs and values. By placing trust in God's plan, I find strength and clarity in my practice, ensuring that my decisions are made with wisdom and compassion. Faith has taught me that success is not just about individual accomplishments but about how I can serve others and contribute to something greater than myself.

How you define success can help you achieve it. If success is purely about financial wealth, then the focus will be on numbers, transactions, and material gains. If success is about living a life of meaning, building relationships, and making a difference, then the journey becomes much richer and more fulfilling. Everyone must determine their definition of success, but it is important to recognize that true success is holistic. It encompasses not just career achievements but also personal growth, faith, relationships, and overall well-being.

Medicine is a challenging but rewarding field. It demands dedication, resilience, and continuous learning. But beyond the technical skills and business strategies, the heart of medicine lies in the relationships built, the lives touched, and the purpose fulfilled. When physicians lead with integrity, compassion, and a commitment to excellence, they achieve a level of success that transcends financial gain. They build a legacy of care, trust, and genuine impact.

The journey to success in medicine is not a straight path, nor is it a destination. It is an ongoing process of growth, adaptation, and self-discovery. There will be obstacles, setbacks, and moments of doubt, but these are part of the journey. Embracing these challenges, learning from them, and continually striving for excellence will lead to a fulfilling and successful career. Remember, some efforts will falter, others will flourish, and the secret is simple: persistence is the path, success the destination. Medicine is more than just a profession; it is a calling, a mission, and a lifelong commitment to serving others. Those who approach it with passion, integrity, and a well-rounded perspective will not only find success but also find true fulfillment in their work and lives.

Roadmap to Success

- *Success in healthcare is multifaceted: There is no one-size-fits-all approach. Success depends on various factors, including location, patient population, provider personality, and market forces.*

- *High-quality care is the foundation: Business strategies cannot replace the need for compassionate, skillful patient care. A successful practice is built on integrity, empathy, and patient trust.*

• *Business acumen is essential: Running a practice today requires more than medical expertise. It requires skills in management, finance, and business strategy, which many healthcare providers lack.*

• *Medical education often overlooks business skills: Physicians are frequently unprepared for the business aspects of medicine due to the lack of business education in medical school and residency.*

• *A well-rounded practice includes diverse revenue streams: Diversifying services (e.g., imaging, physical therapy, outpatient surgery) and building a network of interconnected businesses can support long-term success.*

• *Take Care of Your Patients: Patient care should always be the priority. Quality care leads to trust, patient retention, referrals, and a strong reputation. Don't prioritize operational efficiency at the cost of the patient experience.*

• *Value Your Time: Time is your most precious asset. Delegate, automate, and eliminate low-value tasks to focus on high-value activities. Protect your schedule and set boundaries.*

• *Improve What You Already Do: Innovation isn't always about creating something new. Improve and optimize existing practices, services, and partnerships to develop new opportunities and revenue streams.*

• *Don't Be Afraid to Fail: Fear of failure can hold you back. Failure is a learning opportunity, and taking calculated risks is necessary for growth. Persevere through setbacks to achieve long-term success*

SUCCESS

PARTS, PEOPLE & PRINCIPLES

↑ End of Status Quo   ↑ The Team
↑ Matter of Principle   ↑ Leadership
↑ Stuck in the System   ↑ Final Thoughts

FOUNDATIONS & STRATEGIES

↑ The Right Structure   ↑ You're Worth a Lot
↑ Don't Work for Free   ↑ Play with the Big Boys
↑ Ancillary Streams   ↑ Tech Toys
↑ Let's Make a Deal   ↑ Virtual World
↑ Opportunities   ↑ Providers at All Levels

BACKGROUND & CHALLENGES

↑ Roadmap to Success
↑ The Calling   ↑ The Choices
↑ Sterotypes   ↑ Headaches
↑ Guilt   ↑ The Barriers

ROADMAP
to SUCCESS

Appendix 1

My Story

I grew up in rural western Washington State. My family lived in the foothills overlooking the Snoqualmie Valley. Construction was still ongoing, and forested lots separated the few homes that had been built. The community surrounded a small lake, about a ten-minute walk from my house. Since I didn't live in one of the expensive houses on the lake, I had to walk to the public beach to access the lake.

I spent my free time fishing or playing with friends in the forests. In the summers, I would say goodbye to my mom in the morning, spend the day fishing and playing with friends, and return for dinner at dusk. It was great!

My father worked in the forest industry, so I learned about the outdoors early in life, and like my father, developed a love for the forests. My mother worked off and on, but to my memory was mainly at home raising myself, my brother, and my sisters. My dad slowly transitioned into the corporate office of the company, and due to his hard work, intelligence, and ability to connect with people, he rapidly moved up the corporate ladder. He eventually broke away and started his own company selling investments. For a while, he was successful. I worked for him part-time, mainly sorting and organizing files. Watching my father, I learned the basics of how to run a company, as well as the hard work required to succeed. I also learned the harsh reality of managing people. My father taught me this when he fired me.

During the summer in high school, I had taken advantage of the situation. I didn't put in the expected time, but I still expected a paycheck. Being fired by my father taught me a valuable lesson about work and responsibility. When it happened, I didn't think it was so valuable, but looking back now, I must admit I would have fired myself, too. But the biggest impact on my life did not come from experiencing my father's success, but from his failure.

At the age of forty-six, my father had to file for bankruptcy, and my parents ended up losing everything, including their home. My father-in-law (who was just my girlfriend's father at the time) gave them a place to stay and hired both my mother and father to work at his farm. This was an act of kindness and love I will never forget. While watching my father go through this process, and our family lose everything, I always wondered why my dad chose this path. I realized over time that he chose his integrity, and he chose to restore his customer's money. Even though it put us on the street, he did the right thing. Going through this and watching his decisions ingrained values in me that still guide me today. He did everything he could to provide the best service he could for his clients and to follow through on his commitments. He stood tall and took it on the chin, and did everything he could to make things right.

I also learned from his example how to restart, and sometimes it is better to let things burn to the ground. It is the only way to rebuild. My family's financial transition occurred when I attended college. The life lessons I had learned by watching him shaped me.

He would always challenge me to consider studying medicine or engineering, which held no interest for me. I disliked the sight of blood and felt extremely uncomfortable in any medical situation. However, I believe God had a different plan for me. By providence, I was thrust into multiple medical emergencies. I found myself as the first on the scene of multiple car accidents or people with medical emergencies. Forced to respond in these situations, I provided what little help I could until the ambulance arrived. I felt so helpless in these encounters and started to wish I could do more to help.

I remember one episode during this time when my mother was choking on a hot dog. I got up and ran from the table instead of making any attempt at helping. I was so fearful of these situations that flight was my response. Fortunately, my mother was fine. I believe my father helped her, and the episode ended quickly. But this was the start of a turning point in my journey. I felt so helpless in these situations, especially with my mother, that I knew I needed to address this fear and find a way to be useful in them.

This started my reluctant introduction to medicine. I began by taking some first aid and CPR classes. This gave me some basic knowledge and helped to decrease some of the anxiety I felt in these medical emergency encounters. I had no desire to go further in this field, but the pathway ahead kept leading in that direction.

As a high school student, I was intelligent, but not motivated. I attended high school in a small rural community, and my class had only seventy-five students. The school included grades seven through twelve, combined. I played sports and was of average skill level, but I had a late growth spurt and was 6'4" by the end of my junior year. This gave me some success in basketball at the small-school level. My ambitions at that time were to play in the NBA or be in a rock band. Neither of which I had the talent or the motivation to achieve. My teachers used to complain to my parents during parent–teacher conferences that I would score high on standardized tests, but only get average grades in the classroom. They felt I lacked effort and motivation. As I look back, I can tell you that I was a hard worker and could have done better in both school and athletics. However, at that age and in that small community, where athletes could get away with more than other students, I was a knucklehead.

I was smart enough to find a way to get by with the least amount of effort. That logic got me C's and no athletic opportunities. Although I had a good time and great memories with friends, I'm not sure how much of it I would change. My lackluster effort eventually caught up to me, and with two months to graduation, I had no plan, no college applications, and no idea what to do next. A concerned teacher reached out to my parents and let them know that I had made no plans. My father encouraged me to apply to my local community college, and I was able to enroll for the fall semester. So, at least I had a starting point, but besides completing the basic requirements, I had no idea what to study.

I discussed options with my father, and he suggested engineering. Now, at that time, I had no idea what that entailed. I liked cars and enjoyed fixing and tinkering with them, so I thought designing cars would be cool, which sparked my interest in engineering. I quickly realized what engineering meant: math! This was one subject where I struggled. So off I went, ready to draw pictures of cars, and slammed directly into structural physics, advanced calculus, and fluid dynamics. It did not go well.

I also tried out for the college basketball team. This went okay until about a month into practice, just before final cuts, when the coach asked for grade checks to be submitted for all players. I was unaware that a minimum GPA was required to play on the college team. Due to the classes I was attempting to take and my lack of attention to detail at that time, I was unaware that you could drop a class. Therefore, I received an "F" in one of my engineering classes and missed the deadline to drop the class. So not only did I lose any possible opportunity to play on the basketball team, but I also had that wonderful letter front and center on my permanent transcript. This forever reminded me of where a lack of preparation, planning, and effort will lead.

Thankfully, due to the "F," the college had me meet with an advisor and helped me get on a better path. I stopped pursuing engineering and instead aimed to meet the basic requirements for my AA, which would enable me to be eligible to transfer to a university. I began to improve. As I mentioned earlier, I was intelligent, but not focused. Now that my basketball career had ended, I looked for other things to fill my time. An opportunity arose to shadow a physical therapist. Having had a few sports injuries, I was somewhat familiar with the basics of therapy, which led me to consider it as a possible career.

This was my first big step into the world of healthcare. I enjoyed this. I liked the interaction with patients. Participating in their recovery and treatment was very rewarding. However, I felt somewhat limited. I wasn't the one making the diagnosis or guiding the patient's whole treatment course. I was an important part of the plan, but not the ultimate decision maker. This experience was the door that opened for me to consider a career in medicine.

I completed my AA and was accepted at Washington State University. I began to take pre-med classes to see if medicine might be something in which I was interested. One of these classes was Human Gross Anatomy. I was fortunate at WSU; they had an anatomy class with human cadaver labs and actual dissections. This truly mimicked medical school anatomy cours-es, but just on a condensed scale. I excelled in this class. Something clicked with me, and I seemed to understand this subject. I was very interested in learning how the body was put together and how it worked. I went on to become a teaching assistant in this class.

With this spark of interest, I became motivated in my studies and con-tinued to do well in my other pre-med classes. These subjects just made sense to me, and I had a natural affinity for the biological sciences, which made studying and performing in these subjects somewhat easy. I was able to improve my grades and received nearly straight A's during my time at WSU. I took my MCAT and applied to medical school. Given that I had some blemishes on my transcripts and only average scores on my MCAT, and that I only applied to my in-state school, I did not get in on my first try.

But this was not a setback, but a year of life changes and continued fo-cus on my goal. I got married, worked a "real" job in concrete fabrication, and volunteered in an ER and disability rehab program to gain experience and knowledge of the medical field. After all, I was coming from a starting point of wanting nothing to do with healthcare and needed this time to learn what the medical field was really like.

While both experiences expanded my knowledge base, I was partic-ularly inspired by my time at the rehab program. This program worked with children and adults with severe physical and mental developmental disabilities. It was primarily centered around therapeutic horse riding, but incorporated multiple aspects of physical therapy and mobility into the treatment programs. I will never forget some of my interactions and expe-riences with these patients. The benefits of the treatments to these patients, as well as their smiles and loving appreciation of the help we were provid-ing, allowed me to realize the joy of caring for people.

I reapplied to medical schools and got in this time, and started down the road of healthcare.

The following are a few other highlights of my history that I believe are important to share, as they helped shape my experience.

First, like many married medical students, especially those with children, I relied on student loans to help my family live. The cost of tuition and living expenses leaves most medical students, like myself, with a substantial debt burden upon completing their training. I accumulated over $250,000 in loan debt upon completing my schooling. This is an important factor in the challenges facing most healthcare providers. This debt anchor can make things difficult moving forward in your life and career. Choosing what job or career path to take, where to live, when or if you can buy a house, etc. While these are challenges that face most people, not everyone starts a quarter of a million in the hole.

Second, I was fortunate enough to start my practice with a group of physicians who were not only great people and physicians but also great mentors and business-minded individuals. I learned the business of running a quality, successful medical practice. The founders of this practice taught me how to be an effective leader, navigate the complexities of the healthcare field, and make informed decisions for the practice that enabled the business to grow and thrive. Most importantly, how to provide great care for their patients with compassion and heart.

Their example, as well as that of my father, gave me a firm foundation in the world of business. The reason I share this background is to show you the unique perspective I can have on the field of medicine. I observe the stereotypical types that comprise my colleagues, and I can understand their struggles in achieving success in the healthcare field.

I have been in medicine for over twenty years now. I have been in private practice my entire career. I currently run a large, multiple-specialty practice with my partners. We run an MSO (management service organization) with multiple clients from different areas of healthcare. We own an ambulatory surgical center (my second), a durable medical equipment (DME) supply company, a billing and revenue cycle management company, a family practice group, an urgent care center, a regenerative medicine practice, and operate hospital orthopedic and rehabilitation departments.
These experiences have taught me about the battles and challenges that

we all face in this career, but they have also taught me the pathways to success and fulfillment in medical practice. The field of healthcare can be challenging and always changing, but with these variables, opportunities can be found.

Success is available if you know where to look and how to find it.

www.ingramcontent.com/pod-product-compliance
Lightning Source LLC
Chambersburg PA
CBHW071706210326
41597CB00017B/2354